Fly Fishing
Simple to Sophisticated

SECOND
EDITION

Al Kyte, EdD
University of California, Berkeley

Leisure Press
Champaign, Illinois

Library of Congress Cataloging-in-Publication Data

Kyte, Al.
  Fly fishing, simple to sophisticated.

  Bibliography: p.
  Includes index.
  1. Trout fishing. 2. Fly fishing. I. Title.
SH687.K97 1987   799.1'755   86-27174
ISBN 0-88011-285-9

Developmental Editor: Sue Ingels Mauck
Copy Editor: Lise Rodgers
Assistant Editor: Janet Beals
Production Director: Ernie Noa
Assistant Production Director: Lezli Harris
Typesetter: Brad Colson
Text Design: Keith Blomberg
Text Layout: Denise Peters
Illustrations By: Linnea Wigren
Photographs by: Van Rackages and Scott Henderson
Cover Design: Conundrum Designs
Cover Photo: © 1986 David E. Klutho/Focus West
Printed By: Versa Press

ISBN: 0-88011-285-9

Printed in the United States of America
10 9 8 7 6 5 4 3 2 1
Leisure Press
A division of Human Kinetics Publishers, Inc.
Box 5076, Champaign, IL 61820
1-800-DIAL-HKP
1-800-334-3665 (in Illinois)

Dedication

To George P. Dozier
*Who took the time to pass his love
of fly fishing on to me*

To Barbara, Bertha and Al Kyte, Sr.
*Who cared enough to encourage its
further development*

To John and Tamara
With whom I can share this love

Acknowledgments

To the extent that I am successful in what I have set out to do, I give much of the credit to the combined artistry of Linnea Wigren and Van Rackages. I think you will agree that the essential beauty of Linnea's drawings and the clarity of Van's photographs make it possible for you to visualize some of the more abstract concepts I have tried to communicate. I should also credit Scott Henderson for the black and white photographs of fly patterns I have included in the second edition.

I am indebted to a willing and capable group of angler-editors including Bob Dering, Mel Krieger, Scott Henderson, Frank

Collin, John Fanucchi, and Chet Murphy. The streams they fish are a good deal clearer than the manuscript they waded through.

Over the last 40 years, I have been quite fortunate in the fly fishermen I have known. Their willingness to share their knowledge and skill has undoubtedly contributed to the content of this book. First and foremost was George P. Dozier, a skilled dry fly angler of freestone streams, whom I was fortunate enough to have for my uncle. A great man and an ideal fishing companion, he made the sport a fantastic adventure for a young boy—an adventure that becomes an obligation to transmit to others. In effect, he gave me years of free lessons on reading water and fishing with dry flies.

Others who have personally shared their expertise, in order of their appearance, were Paul Needham (the trout and its environment), Cal Bird (fly tying, fishing spots), E.H. "Polly" Rosborough (fly tying, nymphing, fishing spots), Dick Holland (nymphing, streamer fishing, big fish habits), Ted Fay (wet fly fishing, fishing spots), André Puyans (fly tying, meadow-stream dry fly fishing), Howell Daly and Vince Resh (aquatic entomology), Frank Collin (fly tying, dry fly fishing), Charles Brooks (nymphing, fishing spots), Bob Howe (fly tying, nymphing), Mel Krieger (fly casting, equipment), Hal Janssen (still water fly fishing, equipment modifications), and Bob Giannoni (casting and teaching methods). The personal interaction with these experts has been at least as rewarding as sharing the concepts they have offered.

Other men have contributed important ideas to my fly fishing perspective without making personal appearances. These include Al McClane (perspective on the sport), Jim Leisenring (wet fly fishing), Chuck Fothergill (nymphing), G.E.M. Skues and Frank Sawyer (nymphing), Hartt Wixom (big fish habits), Vince Marinaro (meadow-stream dry fly fishing, fly tying), Al Troth (fly tying), George Harvey (equipment modifications), Lefty Kreh (fly casting and equipment modifications), Brian Clarke (still water fly fishing), and most recently, Joe Humphreys and George Anderson (nymphing), and Dan Byford (streamer fishing).

In a very real sense, you the reader will be learning from these teachers as you read this book and apply its concepts.

Contents

Preface

This is a book about fly fishing—for trout. I have written it for readers much like myself, who stalk the pages of such books for practical fishing ideas, and don't appreciate having to wade through volumes of prose for each tidbit. I enjoy embellished writing but not when mixed with my fly fishing. What this book lacks in personal accounts of battles with huge trout, it should make up for in a logical and concise presentation of fly fishing concepts.

I have organized this book quite differently from most instructional books of fly fishing. Almost universally, such books contain chapters on the obvious dimensions of the sport—the trout, equipment, casting, reading the water, entomology, dry fly fishing, wet fly and nymph fishing, streamer fishing, lake fishing, and playing and landing trout.

This typical organization of other books makes sense, but it's hard to apply in real fishing situations that you and I actually encounter on lakes or streams. Although such handbooks supply information on how to fish, they leave the learner dangling as to *when* to apply *which* techniques or concepts. For example, when you first find yourself fishing in cascading water, which specific comments from the chapter on tackle and rigging apply? Which casting variations are useful? Which of the comments about dry fly or nymph fishing are appropriate? And which of the many problems in playing big fish are most likely to be experienced? The content of other books simply has not been organized to put these elements together for you.

This kind of integrated approach is what my fly fishing students say they have been missing in the instructional books in our sport. It is what I have aimed to provide in writing this book.

I start my "integrated approach" in chapter 2 after providing some basic information on equipment, rigging up, fly casting, the trout and its environment, and fly fishing etiquette. Chapters 2 through 11 each cover one fairly distinctive fly fishing method or practical fishing "program" in sequence from simple to sophisticated, though any such ordering is arbitrary to a degree. The beginning chapters, especially chapters 2 and 3, are quite basic, but the last four or five assume the reader already has some fly fishing experience.

Each chapter is presented in the same way, by means of identical subheadings. Whether each fly fishing method is unique or is similar to other methods becomes apparent through this ordering. The opening paragraphs of each chapter describe the fishing situation, including such elements as water type, problems for the angler, and distinctive characteristics of the trout or its food. Then each method is described in terms of the following subheadings:

- **Rigging adaptations:** modifications or departures from the basic general-purpose rigging described in chapter 1;
- **The approach:** the role of observation, concealment, and angle of approach;
- **Casting techniques:** variations or specialty casts appropriate to the fishing method;
- **Line-handling and fishing techniques:** specific things you do when the fly is in the water;
- **Hooking and landing the fish:** tips on detecting strikes, setting the hook, and playing the trout that may be distinctive to the fishing method;
- **Wading and safety:** wading equipment, wading techniques, and safety concerns pertinent to this method or habitat;
- **Selected readings:** most helpful sources pertaining to the content presented in the chapter.

So the whole idea is to insert a particular piece of content in that part of the book where it is most useful. The tuck cast, for example, is not introduced until I describe a short-line, wet-fly method that is appropriate to its use. If you are a beginning fly fisher, you probably benefit most from this presentation of content *as you need it*. However, if you feel the need to know more about some of the basic concepts, I suggest you use this book as a cross-reference with one or more of the traditional handbooks for beginners. Such books do not include information for experienced fly fishers (as this one does), so they have room for expanded discussions of equipment selection, knot-tying, trout foods, and other basic concepts. For such cross-referencing I recommend Anderson's *The Curtis Creek Manifesto* because it is usually available, inexpensive, and entertaining. Other larger books, such as Joe Brooks' *Trout Fishing*, provide even more thorough coverage of the basic material.

If you are already experienced at fly fishing, you should find the last half of this book more appealing. You have already read chapters on casting, equipment, reading the water, and fishing techniques, and have fished several of the methods described. The material with which to cross-reference this book is already in your head. So the first part of the book will give order to many of the the things you already do, and perhaps enable you to apply them in different situations. The last four or five chapters should give you more advanced concepts to experiment with in your fishing. If you are quite advanced, this book will provide a logical and practical way to convey your skill and knowledge to others.

Preface to Second Edition

I have been greatly encouraged by people's reactions to the first edition of this book. John Gierach, in reviewing it for *Flyfishing* magazine, commented on the "clear and logical" descriptions of "even the more complicated techniques," and Ed Shroeder, in recommending it to his Orvis students, spoke of it as "one of the few instructional books in the sport that doesn't confuse people." André Puyans went even further in describing *Fly Fishing—Simple to Sophisticated* as "the best structured and most practical book available for any individual serious about learning the subject and sport of fly fishing." These kind remarks and others have given me something to live up to in preparing a second edition.

Also gratifying has been the feedback from the people for whom the book was written—the learners. So many of them have remarked that they do tend to visualize particular types of trout water and greatly appreciate having the information they need organized by water type and technique.

For some time I have been looking forward to this opportunity to do a second edition. There are always changes that need to be made and new content and visual material to improve and enhance such endeavors. I have also wanted to further simplify the basic content in the front half of the book yet add detail and conceptualization to the more advanced chapters toward the back. With these dual aims in mind, I have added 64 new or revised illustrations. The appeal of this book to experienced anglers as well as to beginners seems to be one of the things that sets it apart from other instructional guides. Perhaps this is what Charles Brooks was referring to when he wrote that this book "fills a niche not filled by any other."

Chapter 1

Getting Ready

*I*f you are new to the sport of fly fishing, there are things you will need to know before your first day on the water. You will have to know how to select equipment, assemble it, and use it—how to cast. Also, you will profit by knowing something about your quarry, the trout, and its environment, as well as something about fly fishing etiquette. Such basics, which are covered briefly in this chapter, transcend the various styles or methods of fly fishing described throughout the remainder of the book.

If you have not done so already, take a few moments to read the preface. There I've laid out this book's unusual organization and explained how it is intended to assist you—whether you have fly fished before or not.

Selection of Equipment

In this book, I have described a variety of fly fishing methods—some that work best in rather small streams, and others that are definitely big river techniques. Still others pertain to catching trout in lakes. All are methods for catching trout on an artificial fly. No one fly rod will be perfectly suited to all of these methods. However, if you are a beginner with limited funds for purchasing equipment, you may want to select one general-purpose fly rod that will adequately cover this range of habitat.

The *fly rod* I recommend for general trout use is 8-1/2 feet long and is designed to cast a number 6 fly line. If expense is a consideration, I would further suggest that the fly rod be made of fiberglass, though an increasing number of people are discovering that it is fun to fish with graphite because of its light feel. The expense of obtaining a graphite rod (or a fiberglass one for that matter) can be cut considerably by building (finishing) your own rod; your local tackle-shop dealer should be able to get you started.

Many of the better-selling fly rods are built for such general trout use and feature what is termed a "progressive" action. Though stiff in the butt, these rods are progressively more flexible toward the tip. The progressive nature of this flex in the rod's taper contributes to a smoothness in the release of energy from your casting hand out to the moving fly line.

Most of these popular models lose much of their stiffness somewhere near the middle of the rod, and in this sense are called "medium action" rods. They are thought to provide an attractive balance between power and delicate feel. As you will notice later in the book, there are times when what is termed a "fast" rod, with stiffness farther out into the tip section, may serve your fishing needs. You will also notice that there are times when a "slow" rod, with softness farther down into the butt section, is a logical choice.

If you are interested in only a few of the fly fishing methods described here, or in other fly fishing experiences not covered (e.g., steelhead, shad, striped bass methods), or if you are only 11 years old, your general-purpose fly rod may be somewhat different from the one I have described.

What about *reels* for fly fishing? For beginning fly fishers, I recommend a moderately priced, "single action" fly reel (i.e., one complete revolution of the reel's handle rotates the spool one time). You'd be hard pressed to do better than Scientific Anglers/ 3M fly reels in this medium-price range. I like their System 1 Model 789 for general trout use because of its line capacity and durability. I've also had good luck with Martin's MG 7, an inexpensive reel that combines lightness with line capacity. Yet other anglers, whose opinions I respect, prefer different reels in this price range. Most of these reels have adjustable drag mechanisms, which are adequate for the majority of fishing methods described in this book. They should also be large enough to hold a minimum of 50 yards of small-diameter backing line (e.g., braided nylon or dacron squidding line, such as Cortland's Micron) in addition to the fly line. This backing provides the extra line you need when a large fish takes your fly more than a hundred feet downstream and provides a larger diameter on the spool for easier winding.

Some fly reels are much more expensive than the models mentioned above. Though machined to fine tolerances, their cost

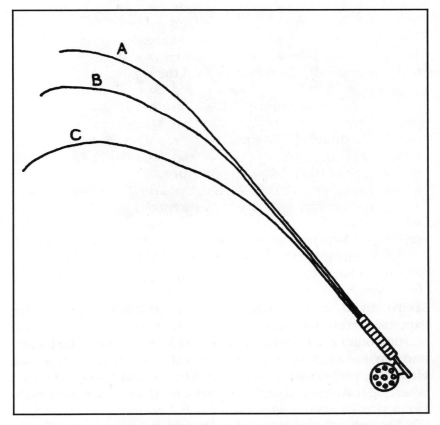

Figure 1.1 Stiffness into the tip section of a working fly rod (A) is associated with fast action, whereas flexibility into the butt (C) means slow action. Most fly rods are classified as medium action (B).

Figure 1.2   Author examines a small Hardy, a well-machined, expensive reel that makes sense when fishing (with delicate tippets) for big trout.

seems out of line with their mechanical simplicity. Some of the expensive reels are fragile, particularly those with an exposed rotating outer rim (used to control drag by pressure of the palm), and become a liability when hit against rocks. (I stumble a lot.) However, well-constructed reels can be important in quiet water when big fish, hooked on fine tippets, move fast enough to over-run a poorly made reel.

Though popular a few decades ago, automatic fly reels are heavy, unreliable, and limited in line capacity. I would use one only if I suffered the misfortune of losing one arm.

When it comes to *fly lines*, I believe it pays to spend the money to buy a quality line—one that lays out smoothly. As of this writing, I am using Cortland (floating) and Scientific Angler (sinking) lines. For a general-purpose first fly line, I recommend a floating, double-tapered (DT), number 6 line to match your rod. The double-tapered line is well suited to the three introductory fishing methods of this book as well as to a number of those that follow. When the enamel inevitably starts to crack on the front taper of your double-tapered line, you can reverse the line on the reel and fish the rear taper. It's like having two fly lines in one. If you are learning on quiet water, consider starting with a weight-forward (WF) line for the reasons discussed in the Rigging Adaptations section of chapter 9.

At the end of your fly line you attach a *leader*, the length of thin monofilament line that forms the almost invisible link between the fly and the thick, highly visible fly line. The tapering down in diameter that begins in the fly line is continued throughout the tapered leader—from its butt at the thick end to its tippet at the small end near the fly. This decrease in the diameter of the line and leader serves to slow the turnover of a cast line and permits your fly to drop gently to the water.

To fish the two most basic fly fishing methods of this book (chapters 2 and 3), you can purchase a nine-foot knotless leader tapered from approximately .021-inch diameter at the butt down to .007-inch (4X) at the tippet. The nine-foot length is long enough to keep the thick fly line some distance away from your fly (and from the fish that approach it) and yet not so long as to make casting difficult.

The 4X or .007-inch diameter indicates how thin the leader tippet is, an important consideration when fishing for leader-shy trout. Usually this is a new concept to people who have fished only with bait and lures and are accustomed to thinking of monofilament only in terms of its strength as measured in pounds test. Usually, the smaller diameters are needed in quiet clear water, where fish have the opportunity to inspect the fly carefully. Here a very thin tippet diameter such as .005 inch (6X) may be necessary to draw strikes. However, fish are seldom leader shy in turbulent water where big weighted flies are cast. In this case a thicker tippet diameter such as .010 inch (1X) might be an excellent choice. If the X number is confusing, you can always subtract it from the constant, 11, to obtain the diameter in thousandths

Figure 1.3   The versatility of the Horner Deer Hair (Humpy) as a dry fly (top) and the Gold-Ribbed Hare's Ear as a sunken fly (bottom) makes them ideal first purchases for the beginner. Start with size 12 flies for riffled water and size 16 for slow water.

of an inch (e.g., 11 − 6X = .005″; 11 − 1X = .010″). This is the so-called "Rule of 11."

One other thing about factory-tapered leaders should be mentioned. The last foot or so of the fine end of the leader is not tapered. As long as you cut only this level portion of the leader when changing flies, there is no major problem. However, in a knotless leader there is no obvious way to tell when you have reached and cut into the thicker tapered portion. When this happens your cast fly begins to land on the water heavily. To avoid this problem, you should cut off the last 18 inches of the fine end of your new tapered leader and replace that piece with 18 to 24 inches of 4X level tippet material. You have made your own leader tippet. Using the leader-to-tippet knot you have just tied as a reference point, you can now see when your tippet becomes too short. If you have changed flies frequently, for example, and have less than 12 inches of tippet left, you have lost much of its strength-

Figure 1.4   Small, plastic boxes lined with strips of self-stick adhesive foam (from Dr. Scholl's Foot and Shoe Padding) provide an inexpensive, protected, and flexible system for carrying trout flies.

giving stretch and should replace it with a new 18- or 24-inch tippet.

Leaders themselves form an esoteric area in the fly fishing world and can become complicated as you begin to fish different methods on a variety of water types (e.g., riffles, pocket water, glides, still water). Throughout the book I will suggest various leaders that are suited to specific functions (fishing methods), and in chapter 10 I will suggest a "loop system" to facilitate making changes from one leader length to another.

As you become addicted to fly fishing, you will find yourself beginning to accumulate accessory equipment that is sold in tackle shops. A few bare-bones essentials to start with besides rod, reel, and line include fishing license, nail clippers (e.g., "Trim" brand) to cut leader material, a container or fly box to hold extra flies, extra leaders and tippet material, and fly flotant. If you wish to kill fish to eat, you'll need a pocket knife and "arctic" creel. Fishing is often less painful if you carry insect repellent, sun-block cream, and dark glasses. Eventually the growing pile of accessories requires the purchase of a vest to hold and organize such items for use.

The flies and wading equipment you decide to use vary with the type of water and the way you fish it. Therefore, they are discussed later in the book.

Assembling the Equipment—Rigging Up

The salespeople in many of the better fly fishing shops are trained to attach the backing to the reel, the fly line to the backing, and the leader to the fly line. Where this service is provided, you are able to observe what is involved in putting your line on correctly. This service also simplifies your early preparations at a time when you are being deluged with new terms and concepts. As a result, you may need to learn only two simple knots when first on the stream. On the other hand, if you like to do things for yourself, most of the basic fly fishing handbooks provide adequate detail in rigging up your line and leader.

The knot you will need to use most often on the stream or lake is one that will attach your fly to the tippet. I have taught long enough to realize that the most important requirement for a knot used by beginning students is that it be easy to tie. The improved clinch knot combines ease of tying with reasonable strength. Though I often use other knots to attach my fly, and refer to them later in this book, I still revert to this one when in a hurry.

The second most necessary knot when fishing is one used to connect a new tippet to the leader. Here again simplicity and reliability have led me to recommend the surgeon's knot. For years I had used only the blood knot to join sections of monofilament and initially resisted a friend's suggestion that I try the surgeon's knot. (I'm sure my reluctance was reinforced by the fact that my friend seldom caught many fish.) Finally he challenged me to see which knot I could tie faster. My fingers were well-practiced at tying blood knots and cranked one out in 30 seconds. After a little instruction and practice on tying the surgeon's knot, these same fingers clumsily completed this unfamiliar task in only 18 seconds. I was impressed. Subsequent

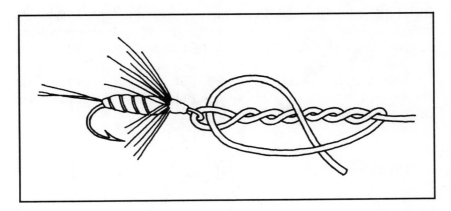

Figure 1.5 Tying the improved clinch knot is easier than it reads:

1. Thread the end of the tippet through the eye of the hook.
2. Wrap this tippet end around the standing part of the leader 5 times and insert it back through the loop in front of the hook eye.
3. Then bring the end back through the big loop just formed.
4. Moisten and tighten the knot steadily and trim its tag end.

reading informed me that this knot can also be used to join leader sections of dissimilar diameters and that it holds better than the blood knot on the newer, stronger tippet materials (e.g., Aeon) that were just beginning to appear in fly shops.

Though the surgeon's knot is the obvious choice as a first knot, you may want to learn the blood knot when ready to complicate life for yourself. I use it when making my own knotted leaders (particularly in the leader's butt section) and when adding a dropper strand to fish two flies at once.

Sooner or later you will need to tie a new leader onto your fly line. If you are meticulous by nature, you probably will be drawn to the beauty and neatness of a knot known as the needle knot. However, I prefer the nail knot because it is as reliable as the needle knot and much quicker to tie. This is important to me in teaching because I must often replace several leaders in a very few moments. The nail knot illustration I have included here shows a tying method that is faster than the one typically found in fly fishing books. However, this faster method will not work if the section of leader being attached to the line has knots in it.

Figure 1.6 The hat trick: Protecting the reel from grit when rigging up is accomplished by placing your hat beneath it.

Now you are ready to finish rigging up for casting practice. Plan to practice at least several times before you go fishing. It will make your first experience on the stream far more enjoyable. A good place to practice casting is in the middle of a grass field free of overhead wires with at least 30 feet of space in front of and behind you. If casting pools and instructors are available, so much the better.

Before assembling the fly rod a little paraffin from a candle stub can be applied to the male ferrule (where the sections of the fly rod connect). Then you twist (don't twist bamboo) these sections together so the guides for the line are all on the same side of the rod. Attach the reel so that the guides and the reel are on the underside of the rod as it is held out in front of you. The line, coming off the bottom of the reel spool, should feed straight out toward the rod tip.

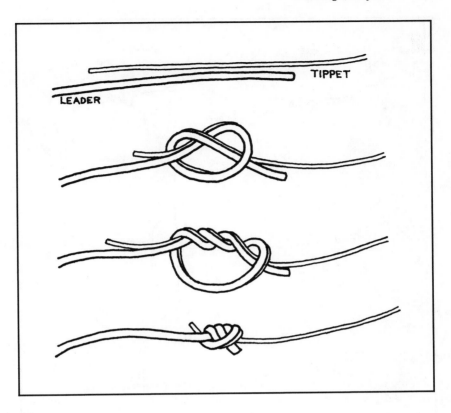

Figure 1.7 Start the surgeon's knot by laying the free end of the leader along-side one end of the tippet so they overlap by 6 to 8 inches. Then each hand holds one end of this doubled strand. The overhand knot is tied with the hand that has the tippet hanging from it. When tippet (and end of leader) have been passed through the loop twice, the knot can be completed by moistening, tightening, and trimming.

Whenever you "rig up" on gravel or dirt, and have to set your reel (and rod) down, place your hat or other object on the ground under the reel to protect it from the grit. Next, strip a couple of yards of line off the reel, fold the end of the fly line back on itself, and thread it out through the guides. If you push the doubled fly line (rather than the end of the leader) out through the guides, the line will not slip back down through the guides if accidentally let go.

Kinks in the leader can be removed by pulling it between your thumb and forefinger under some pressure (i.e., stretching

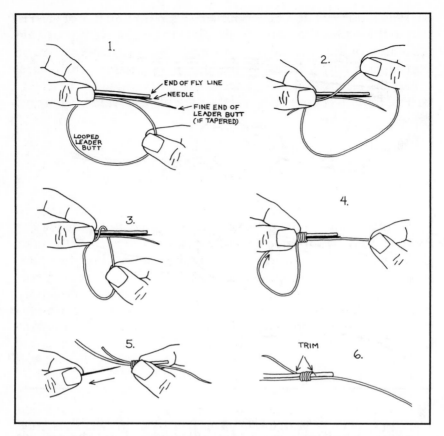

Figure 1.8 Nail knot simplified: This quick-and-easy version of the nail knot requires a knotless leader butt.

1. Form a closed loop with the entire leader piece so both ends cross on top (alongside the fly line and something rigid such as a nail). If the leader butt is tapered, the small end should extend out beyond the end of the fly line.
2. Grasp the loop as pictured with your tying hand and start to wrap it around the nail, fly line, and leader that are being held together.
3. Wrap progressively back *toward* your holding hand until five wraps have been completed.
4. While securing these wraps with your holding hand, grasp the end of the leader that extends beyond the fly line and pull on it until the loop has disappeared.
5. Remove the nail and tighten the knot by pulling on the ends alternately and then simultaneously.
6. Trim the ends as pictured, making sure to angle cut the end of the fly line. Then coat the knot with light-weight, flexible cement such as Sally Hansen's *Hard-as-Nails*.

it). Watch out you don't cut yourself. Finally a tiny tuft of yarn is tied to the end of the tippet to simulate the slight weight and air resistance of the artificial fly. This yarn also stabilizes the end of your tippet, and reduces the likelihood of your being whipped across the face with it. When casting with an actual fly attached, be sure to protect your eyes and the back of your head by wearing glasses and a hat.

Basic Fly Casting Theory

Casting, or throwing the line, is an important part of many forms of angling. In the popular sport of spin fishing, the weight to be cast is concentrated in a lure, which is propelled through the air like a bullet; thus the lure pulls the line out. Just the opposite is true in fly casting, where the line pulls the lure (fly) out. Here the weight to be cast is distributed throughout a thick fly line, which unrolls on itself when cast, pulling a relatively weightless fly along behind. This difference in mechanics of the two casts is reflected in the way they are executed; the spin cast is a relatively sudden, explosive movement, whereas the fly cast is more prolonged, continuous, and controlled.

This unrolling of line in fly casting places the emphasis on linear characteristics of the movement. The fly line starts extended straight in front of you on the ground (water). In what is termed the "back cast," the line is drawn up and back so that it unrolls until straightened in the air behind the rod tip. Then the line is pulled forward again, unrolled to straighten in the air in front, before being dropped to the practice field (or water) in the forward cast. The linear component is evident in that the line straightening behind you is separated by approximately 180 degrees from its straightened position in front of you a second or two later.

To accomplish this straight flow of fly line, the tip of the rod should also be moved in a straight line as the power is being applied. This straight movement of the rod tip results from moving your hand smoothly along a similar but lower path. With short casts, your hand should move in a line that angles upward as well as backward (during the back cast) and then downward as well as forward (during the forward cast). Keep your wrist firm during these movements so the rod will bend against the resistance of the line. When you stop the movement, the power built

Figure 1.9   Drawing the hand forward in a smooth, continuous manner loads the rod properly.

up by bending or "loading" the rod is released, the rod tip reverses its bend, and a "loop" is formed in the moving fly line.

In a well-formed casting loop, the line that extends out from the rod tip is parallel to and beneath the part that is still moving (and hasn't yet turned over). Though it is tempting to see how much line you can cast, your first priority should be to throw well-shaped loops with only 25 to 30 feet of line. You should extend your range only when some measure of loop control has been achieved.

If your line fails to straighten out when casting, the chances are you are making the common beginner's error of bending your wrist instead of the rod. When this happens your rod tip moves in an arc, which completely disrupts the linear relationships and destroys the cast.

The Basic Overhead Cast

In this chapter I am confining my comments to the basic overhead cast. Other casts may be thought of as variations of the over-

Figure 1.10   The parallel loop: When the moving portion of your fly line is parallel to the stationary portion below it, you have achieved a measure of loop control.

head cast, and are introduced later where they apply to particular fishing methods.

Casting is a difficult skill, especially when learning solely from a book. So, I recommend that you seek out a skilled casting instructor and benefit from personal guidance. Frequently such help is available where fly fishing clubs or fly fishing shops exist.

Let's assume that you are back at your practice field, rigged up, and ready to cast. Start with 25 to 30 feet of line beyond the rod tip laid out on the grass in front of you. Grip the rod handle with your casting hand as you might hold a screwdriver; your index finger and thumb should be the same distance up the handle with the thumb toward the top. If this is not comfortable, vary the grip slightly. Use only your casting or "rod hand" for now by trapping the line under the first or second finger. The use of the noncasting or "line hand" is best introduced later, when you have had time to concentrate on what the rod and rod hand should be doing. An improperly used line hand can detract from the way the rod should feel.

In executing the pick-up and lay-down, or water cast, you pick-up or lift the line off the grass (water) with your back cast, pausing for the line to straighten behind you. Then you make the forward cast, which lays the line down on the grass again in front. The numbers below correspond to those in the accompanying illustrations, which are based on tracings of high speed photographs of a fly rod's movement.

The Back Cast

1. *Start low.* At the start of the back cast the rod tip is held low, so it will begin to bend or load as early as possible. If you load the rod late, by starting off with a high tip, you may feel the need to continue the stroke too far in back, which drops the line too low behind you.
2. *Move the line.* As you begin to move the line toward you on the grass by moving the rod butt upward and back, the rod begins to load in the flexible tip section.
3. *Speed up.* As your hand begins to move faster, the rod loads farther down into the butt section. In a long cast, the flex would be more pronounced than that shown in the drawing. Excessive wrist action at this time can throw the rod tip back early and drop the line too low behind you.
4. *Stop.* As the flex of the rod starts rolling back out toward the tip, the hand stops the rod butt. It is often helpful to combine the cues, ''Speed up and Stop,'' as Lefty Kreh does in his teaching. Where this acceleration and stop occurs sets the direction for the continued backward movement of the line. A friend can be of great help to you by watching your back cast from the side and telling you the direction the line is moving back, whether it is straightening, and what the loop looks like (i.e., shape, size).
5. If the rod has been loaded and stopped as described, it should bend back rather than downward after straightening.
6. *Drift.* Once the rod has been stopped, you can loosen your wrist and tip the rod back a little without causing the line

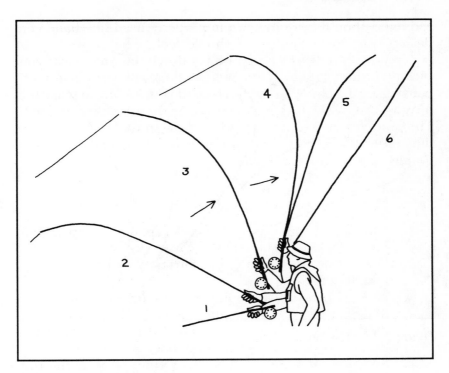

Figure 1.11   The back cast.

to drop. This backward and upward "drift" of the casting hand repositions the rod for full loading of the forward cast. Such repositioning is not needed with short casts, so for simplicity's sake, this drift step should probably be omitted when teaching beginners. It can easily be introduced when a caster is ready to handle the additional line weight of somewhat longer casts.

The Forward Cast

7. *Pause.* It is usually necessary to pause briefly at the completion of the back cast to allow the line to straighten behind you before starting the forward cast. How long you pause depends on how much line is being straightened; additional line requires extra time. When first learning, you may benefit by taking an occasional glance back over your

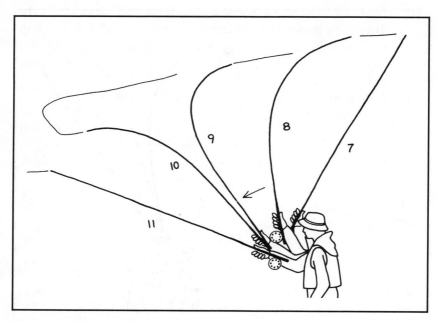

Figure 1.12   The forward cast.

casting shoulder to see for yourself when to start forward.
8. *Pull the butt.* When the line has almost straightened to
    the rear, you begin the forward cast by starting to move
    your hand (and rod butt) forward. Start this movement
    slowly to allow the fly line to begin moving smoothly.
    Applying power prematurely with a sudden wrist move-
    ment during this loading phase causes the tailing loop
    that frustrates so many otherwise skillful fly fishermen.
9. *Put a loop in the rod.* Mel Krieger's phrase catches the es-
    sence of what should happen as you speed up the move-
    ment in applying power. As you speed up, try to think of
    "pulling the rod tip around" as illustrated in the sequence
    from numbers 8 through 10 in the drawing. Though the
    tip is pulled through a considerable distance during this
    time, notice how little the hand moves. It's not unlike
    snapping a towel in the sense that the rapid acceleration
    and sudden stop of the hand serve to generate speed at
    the far end of the towel (or fly rod).

10. *Stop.* As the rod tip turns over, the loop forms in the fly line and progresses out from the rod until all the line has unrolled. Stop the rod tip high to achieve a tight, narrow loop, or stop it somewhat lower when a wider loop seems better.

11. *Follow down.* After the stop and as the last of the line unrolls forward, you continue to lower the rod to achieve a gentle drop of the fly to the grass (water). Lowering the rod in this way after the cast also enables you to return to the low tip position preferred for starting the next back cast.

Throughout this discussion I have emphasized the progressive nature of the loading of a fly rod. I have done so because I think it is an important concept that has not received enough attention in the casting literature.

I think we sometimes get sidetracked by relatively unimportant differences of style in casting techniques. Some of us differ in recommended stances, grips, hand and elbow positions, and uses of the wrist. Even our most respected casting instructors—people like Mel Krieger, Joan Wulff, Lefty Kreh, and Harry Wilson—have different casting and teaching styles. However, the important thing is that they all succeed in getting their students to bend the rod properly so that line will lay out smoothly. That is what fly casting is all about.

False Casting

The false cast is so named because the line isn't allowed to drop to the water to be fished; in this sense it's not the real thing. When false casting, you start a back cast just as the line is about to straighten in front of you but before it has had time to fall to the water. False casts are used to work out additional line, measure the amount of line in relation to your target, change the direction of your cast, and dry off your fly. False casting should be practiced as should the pick-up and lay-down, because both are used in fishing and both require different casting planes. Because the false cast starts with the line in the air in front of you (rather than on the ground), there isn't as much opportunity to lift the line in back. Therefore the casting plane is more horizontal.

Adding the Line Hand

Though we have been casting with the "rod hand" only, you probably are aware that the line is held in the noncasting or "line hand" when casting to catch fish. When you first add the line hand to your practice casting, you should hold it down near your stomach to make sure the line is "anchored" away from the rod. If this is not done and your line hand moves up near the rod, you may be feeding line into the cast and interfering with the loading of the rod.

When you learn to double haul with the line hand (as introduced in chapter 6), you will know how to tighten the line with little tugs during both the back cast and the forward cast.

The Trout and Its Environment

There is more to fishing than equipment and casting. This becomes evident when you watch beginning anglers casting about indiscriminately as if the trout must be everywhere. Most of us learn from experience that trout are not randomly or evenly distributed in a lake or stream. In order to have an idea of where to fish, you need to know something about the trout and its aquatic environment. Some of this basic information is presented here because it holds true regardless of the fishing method you use.

First of all, trout are found in cold water. They are thought to be able to survive in water between 40 and 80 degrees F., but usually feed within a more restricted range. Joe Humphreys, a knowledgeable Eastern fly fisher and teacher, is among those who build a strong case for the importance of water temperature and the use of a water thermometer. I have found temperature readings to be most valuable early in the season and again during the heat of late summer. In the spring, a reading may tell me whether or not the water has become warm enough to activate the fish. Late in the summer I need to find out if the water has become too warm for the trout to feed normally. Thus these readings may be a great time saver by telling me to fish elsewhere.

The content of oxygen in water also determines where fish may hold. In well-aerated water, the supply of oxygen is seldom a problem for trout, but high temperature, acidity, excessive weed-growth, and pollution can all work to deplete oxygen supply. When this happens, for example, as a result of hot summer weather, trout may be forced to move to the most aerated riffles.

Usually, however, trout are found where they are safe from predators. This safety comes from the overhead cover afforded by large rocks, logs, weed beds, deep water, undercut banks, or riffled water. In *The Ecology of Running Waters*, Hynes characterizes mountain streams as alternating deep and shallow areas—deep basins and riffles. The depth of the basins, the choppy surface of the riffles, and any large midstream rocks provide much of the trout's cover. Hynes characterizes meadow streams by the meandering nature of their channels, which have a "regularity of curving pattern, regardless of stream size." Wherever the main current intersects a bank, it has the potential to erode out a deep, undercut area. Trout use these areas and midstream weed beds for cover in this type of water.

Even when trout feed in the shallows, they are seldom far from the protection of deeper water. In lakes, for example, they frequently cruise the shoreline close to where it drops off sharply. The food is generally abundant in the shallow areas where water plants thrive, but protection is found in deep water beyond the drop-off.

A trout's safety is enhanced by its well-developed sensory organs. With independent, protruding eyes on each side of its

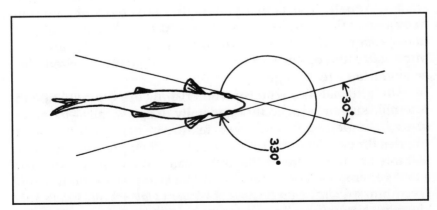

Figure 1.13   The sight-gifted trout's only blind spot is directly in back. This vision is important to predation as well as protection, because the trout is a sight hunter.

head—eyes that can move in their sockets—a trout can see in all directions, with the exception of the 30 degrees directly behind it. These fish can also detect vibrations and pressure differences in the water in excess of 50 feet under quiet conditions. Therefore you may need to keep low, tread quietly, avoid loud colors in your clothing, and generally stalk or hunt your fish.

Specific information on "reading the water," or studying it to determine where trout should be holding, is available in many books. Charles Brooks' *The Trout and the Stream* and *Larger Trout for the Western Fly Fisherman* remain two of my favorites. Gary Borger has a well-organized chapter on trout lies in *Nymphing—A Basic Book*, in which he seems to build on material developed by Hynes. What I do in the following chapters of this book is describe specific water types as part of the fishing situation that sets the stage for each method of fishing.

Where trout are found is frequently where food is available. In streams, trout face upcurrent and see food that drifts downstream toward them. Sometimes they feed without moving from their protected "lies." Other times they must leave this "holding water" to find food, either by foraging along the bottom or stationing themselves in nearby "feeding water" where drifting food is concentrated. As previously mentioned, trout in lakes frequently cruise along the shoreline to find food.

Most pan-sized trout feed on insects, both land-born (terrestrial) and aquatic. Land insects such as ants, beetles, leafhoppers, and grasshoppers sometimes get blown into the water and drift downstream. Aquatic insects that you might know by their common names—mayflies, caddisflies, stoneflies, dragonflies, damselflies, midges—are eaten under water in immature nymph, larva, or pupa states and on the surface as they emerge into winged flies or alight later to lay eggs.

The artificial flies you use when fishing are typically tied to resemble such insects—either generally or specifically—in terms of size, shape, color, and even texture. Chapters 3 and 4 of Charles Brooks' *Nymph Fishing for Larger Trout* provide an excellent introduction to insect life in the water. If you are looking for a first general book on what I would term angler's entomology, I recommend *The Complete Book of Western Hatches* by Hafele and Hughes, *Naturals* by Borger, or *Guide to Aquatic Trout Foods* by Whitlock. The main focus of this book, however, is on learning how to fish, so insects are mentioned only in their obvious associations with particular fly patterns, aquatic habitat, or fishing methods.

Fly Fishing Etiquette

"Good manners" means different things in different fishing situations. One thing it almost always means is to avoid doing anything to disturb another angler's fishing water. To me this applies not only to the water an angler is casting into at the moment, but also the water he or she will be casting into during the next half hour. This can be estimated by watching the direction and rate of movement of the angler who has arrived ahead of you at your favorite "hot spot." So good manners may mean walking for 20 minutes before fishing to avoid disturbing a fast-moving angler. Or in the case of a slow-moving angler, it may mean leaving several big pools undisturbed. It may mean selecting a spot at least one normal cast (50 feet) to the side of a stationary meadow-stream fly fisher. If you don't know if your presence will disturb someone, ask.

By now you must be ready to move on to the business of fishing. You know enough about equipment, casting, and trout for the time being.

Selected Readings

Anderson, S. (1976). *The Curtis Creek manifesto*. Portland, OR: Salmon Trout Steelheader.

Brooks, J. (1972). *Trout fishing*. New York: Harper & Row.

Helleckson, T. (1977). *Popular fly patterns*. Salt Lake City: Peregrine Smith.

Kreh, L., & Sosin, M. (1972). *Practical fishing knots*. New York: Crown.

Leiser, E. (1978). *The complete book of fly tying*. New York: Alfred A. Knopf.

Scientific Anglers. (1977). *Fly fishing handbook* (1st ed.). Midland, MI: Scientific Anglers.

Basic Casting

Green, J. (1971). *Fly casting . . . from the beginning*. Westminster, CA: Fenwick/Sevenstrand.

Krieger, M. (1979, Early Season). Understanding the casting arc. *Fly Fisherman*.

Krieger, M. (1981, Summer). An introduction to fly casting. *The Flyfisher*.

Krieger, M. (1984). *The essence of flycasting* [60-minute VHS video-tape]. Sebastopol, CA: Sonoma Video Productions.

The Trout and Its Environment

Borger, G. (1979). *Naturals*. Harrisburg, PA: Stackpole.

Borger, G. (1979). *Nymphing—A basic book*. Harrisburg, PA: Stackpole.

Brooks, C.E. (1970). *Larger trout for the western fly fisherman*. New York: A.S. Barnes.

Brooks, C.E. (1974). *The trout and the stream*. New York: Crown.

Brooks, C.E. (1976). *Nymph fishing for larger trout*. New York: Crown.

Hafele, R., & Hughes, D. (1981). *The complete book of western hatches*. Portland, OR: Frank Amato.

Humphreys, J. (1981). *Joe Humphreys' trout tactics*. Harrisburg, PA: Stackpole.

Hynes, H.B.N. (1970). *The ecology of running waters*. Toronto: University of Toronto Press.

Needham, P.R. (1969). *Trout streams*. New York: Winchester.

Whitlock, D. (1982). *Guide to aquatic trout foods*. New York: Winchester.

Chapter

Fishing Down and Across Stream With a Wet Fly: Starting Simply on Moving Water

A wide riffle is an ideal type of water in which to learn the basic down and across wet fly method. The riffle should be wide enough to permit a 20- to 30-foot cast directly across stream. The choppy, riffling nature of the water's surface helps to conceal you from the trout, minimizing the need for a quiet approach and splash-free cast. The wading, which can be traumatic to some beginners, is seldom difficult in shallow, gravel-bottomed riffles. Even the across-stream cast simplifies learning by presenting the fly on a line that is tightening as it moves downstream away from you. This tight line enables you to experience some early success by hooking trout that wouldn't be felt or caught on a slack line.

Riffles have another important feature. They harbor a wide variety of small animals that trout eat. The gravel and larger rocks on the bottom provide cover for small, immature insects such as

Figure 2.1   Impressionistic nymphs such as a Gold-Ribbed Hare's Ear resemble a variety of immature aquatic insects.

mayfly nymphs and caddis larvae as well as larger predators that seek them out, including stonefly nymphs, dragonfly nymphs, small fish (e.g., sculpin), and crayfish. Trout frequently use riffles as "feeding water."

Rigging Adaptations

The basic, general-purpose fly fishing equipment described in the first chapter will serve you well in fishing these riffles. A useful consideration when initially faced with the problem of selecting a fly is to obtain a few weighted patterns that represent a wide variety of the insect life that trout feed on. A popular, readily available wet fly or nymph that does this is the Gold-Ribbed Hare's Ear nymph; it loosely resembles several common forms of aquatic life, including some mayfly nymphs, caddisfly larvae and caddisfly pupae. Tied in a size 10 or 12 with about 6 turns of 2-amp lead-fuse wire under the body material, this fly is large enough to attract the trout's attention in choppy water and heavy enough to reach many of the bottom currents where trout most often lie. Where the water is less turbulent, a smaller, less-weighted size 14 Hare's Ear is better.

A 9-foot leader, tapered down to 4X, is a good starting point for fishing the wide riffles associated with this basic method.

After a while you'll probably notice that your fly doesn't always land on the water as gently as you think it should. Maybe you have tied on a fly that is either too heavy or too light for the tippet you are using. In order to avoid this problem and properly match your fly size to tippet diameter, it is helpful to refer to the fly fisher's "rule of three." According to this rule, you determine the size "X" tippet to use by dividing the selected fly size by 3. As an example, suppose you decide that stream conditions warrant the use of a number 12 fly. You divide 12 by 3 as the rule directs you and tie on a 4X tippet. Eventually you deviate from this guideline slightly as you encounter fly patterns that are unusually heavy or light for their hook size.

The Approach

Before you start to fish, why not sample the stream bottom for insects? Find out which insects are abundant in that section of stream. When you learn to recognize various types of aquatic insects, you begin to understand why certain artificial flies look the way they do. You begin to know when to use particular fly patterns.

An effective screen for collecting insects can be made by stapling a piece of window screen (i.e., 2 feet high by 3 feet across) between two poles or sticks (e.g., old broom sticks). The bottom of the screen should be almost flush with the bottom of the poles to prevent insects from escaping underneath. You place the screen downstream of a likely-looking rock and hold it there while you lift up the rock. Insects that swim or drift away are swept into your screen, while those that cling to the rock can be picked off by hand. This collecting should not be done where it will disturb the actual area you will be fishing.

The most common error in insect collecting is to sample from one aquatic habitat only. Be sure to sample from slow as well as fast currents, from sand and gravel as well as rubble bottom,

Figure 2.2   Sampling the stream bottom tells you what aquatic life is abundant there and provides ideas for fly patterns.

and from submerged sticks and aquatic vegetation as well as rocks.

I have indicated that the water selected for this method of fly fishing should be wide enough and turbulent enough to permit you to use an across-stream cast without spooking fish. Because it's not always apparent where fish are lying in a riffle, or how many fish are feeding there, you should cover such water systematically. The most common approach is to wade in at the head of the riffle (upstream end). Your first casts are made from the

Figure 2.3   Some forms of aquatic life cling to rocks while other forms drift or swim into the downstream-held screen.

shore at times to avoid spooking trout that may be holding in the shallow water close to you. Generally you fish the near water with a short line, then when the line has been extended, you cover the water farther out. Next, you move a few steps downstream and repeat this near-to-far sequence. This procedure is repeated until the riffle has been fished from head to tail.

In many streams your success will depend on the time of day you select to fish. This point was brought home to me vividly one June evening some years ago. My friend Dick Holland and

Figure 2.4 Dropping to one knee provides concealment for the first, short casts at the head of a riffle.

I drove all day and weren't able to start fishing till 7:30 pm. I had the only car key and didn't want Dick to have to wait for me, so I quit fishing at nine o'clock. It turns out we had each caught three modest-sized trout by that time. But while I walked back to the car, Dick continued to fish. In the extra half hour, he hooked four more fish—all substantially larger than those we caught from the same water before 9:00 pm.

A week later I checked this time-of-day effect on a heavily fished riffle of another stream. I had watched several anglers fish it that day and take a total of two rainbow trout between 6 and 8 inches long. That evening, on my first cast, I caught a 15-inch brown trout—a species known to adapt particularly well to the presence of daytime anglers by feeding at night. And that riffle had a large log off to one side, which provided excellent daytime cover for a decent fish. It's always a good idea when approaching a riffle to make note of obvious cover. Then, if it's feasible, return to fish the riffle again just before dark. You may be pleasantly surprised.

When fishing big rivers I constantly keep an eye out for shallow, wide riffles off to one side of deep heavy runs. Some of these riffles are wide and long enough to cover an extensive area of stream bottom. And this type of bottom is ideally suited to many species of aquatic insects. On a summer evening thousands of insects may emerge from a single riffle. The deep, heavy water off to the side provides daytime cover for large trout—often a surprising number of large trout. Under the cover of dusk, these trout sometimes move into the shallow riffles to feed voraciously while expending very little energy. When insects are emerging in large numbers, this may be the trout's only feeding time.

Casting Techniques

All that is required of you as a beginning angler in this method is to be able to cast a fly line a distance of up to 30 feet. At the end of each drift the fly is well downstream of you and is returned back upstream by means of a false cast or two. Such false casts also enable you to extend line when necessary.

Line-Handling and Fishing Techniques

Immediately after the cast, the line being held in your line hand should be brought over to your rod hand and hooked in the index or second finger of that hand (the finger used is a matter of personal preference). This finger of the rod hand becomes the point at which you maintain control of the drifting line. Then any retrieving of line can be done most easily by the line hand's pulling in or "stripping in" line a few inches at a time from behind this control point.

The most common problem beginners have with this sequence is in learning which hand to move to the other when hooking the line onto the rod hand. Instead of bringing the line hand over to the rod hand as they should, many beginners have a tendency to move their dominant hand and thus start bringing the fly rod over to the line hand. Also it helps to remind some beginners to "cast with your hands apart and fish with your hands together" when practicing this maneuver.

After the cast has been made, the line and fly drift downstream. Should part of the line lead the fly downstream, it creates a curve or belly on the water that begins to pull the fly across

Figure 2.5   Stripping in line begins by grasping it just behind and below where it is controlled by the rod hand.

stream unnaturally fast, thus disrupting a natural drift. When this happens, you should lift some of the fly line off the water and place it down again in a different alignment, most often a little farther upstream. This line-handling technique, the upstream mend, is accomplished by lifting the rod tip and moving it upstream whenever the drifting line starts to overtake the fly. The line may have to be mended several times during the same drift. With proper mending, the entire drifting portion of the fly line remains a little upstream of the fly, which allows the fly to sink and drift downstream naturally.

As soon as the line is mended, you should return the tip of the fly rod to a low position over the water and let it follow the fly throughout the remainder of its drift. At the moment the fly line straightens, the drifting fly will begin to lift off the bottom and start its swing across stream. It is at this time more than any other that the trout is likely to grab your fly. To a trout following your fly, this sudden change in movement seems to signal that a meal is about to escape.

A retrieve may not be necessary on very short casts, but on long casts it is a convenient means of recovering enough line

Figure 2.6   The line is stripped or pulled down a few inches. It is then released to fall toward the water as the line hand returns upward to make the next strip.

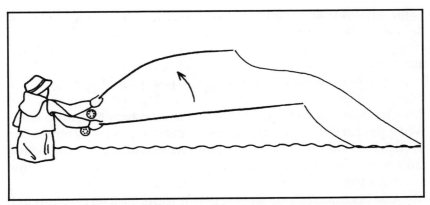

Figure 2.7   Mending line involves lifting the floating part off the water and placing it down again off to whichever side affords an improved drift.

from the water to be able to cast again. Sometimes fish that have ignored your drifting fly will strike as it is being actively retrieved upstream. As previously indicated, the simplest and most common way to retrieve line is to strip it in with the line hand from

Figure 2.8   Fishing the drift with line moving downstream from left to right and rod pointed toward the fly.

behind the rod hand. As the line comes in, hold it in loose loops or just let it fall on the water.

Hooking and Landing the Fish

There are different schools of thought on how to set the hook when a trout takes your fly. To some extent these different techniques depend on the fly fishing method and water type being fished. This will become more apparent as you read some of the chapters that follow.

As a beginning fly fisher you may find yourself so preoccupied with casting, knot-tying, and line-handling that you fail to give much thought to how the hook should be set. If the hook is set at all on your first few fish, it is probably a natural-tendency technique of lifting the hand, arm, and fly rod, often with excessive force. Lifting the fly rod continues to serve you well in some methods, though many experienced fly fishers begin to rely increasingly on the line hand to do at least part of this job. Typically you pull down with the line hand as you lift the rod.

Figure 2.9 Mending or lifting the floating line off the water is done to reposition it in better alignment with the fly. Here the line will be replaced farther upstream.

The whole idea in setting the hook is to tighten the line and move the fly enough to allow penetration of the hook into the trout's jaw. The more slack line that is on the water, the more pronounced your movements of rod tip and/or line hand must be to achieve this tightening. There is a fine line between too much and too little force to set the hook. This comes with experience.

Once the fish has been hooked, the most important thing at this level of angling is to keep the line tight. Should the fish move toward you, this tightness can be maintained by stripping line in as discussed in the previous section on retrieving. If wading, you can slowly and carefully wade back to shore, leading the fish in that direction while it is still under water. If fishing without a net, you may decide to slide a large trout up a gently sloping part of the shoreline.

If the fish is small and you want to release it, you can bring it directly in to you at midstream. At times you will be able to release it by touching only the hook—turning it so the point of the hook is down. When you do this, trout sometimes fall off the hook as a result of their own movements. Surgical hemostats

Figure 2.10 Watching a healthy trout swim away and knowing you haven't depleted a fishery brings satisfaction.

may be carried to remove deeply embedded hooks. The most common error I see in watching people play trout is the tendency to keep the fish on the hook much longer than necessary, thus exhausting the fish and diminishing its chances for survival. Whenever you release a large trout, remember to handle it gently without squeezing and place it in the water facing upstream. Watch to make sure the gills are functioning properly. Gradually loosen your hold to check whether or not it can maintain an upright, balanced position in the water. When it has recovered, the fish should be able to swim out of your hold.

Such catch-and-release fishing is the best single management tool we have to assure a continued supply of healthy, wild trout. It is best done with barbless hooks, or hooks that have had the barb pressed down to contribute to a higher survival rate. Most anglers expect to lose their fish when first switching to barbless hooks. It's amusing to see their reaction when this doesn't happen. If you are like most of us, you will feel sheepish about not having switched sooner. The trend is to fish barbless.

Figure 2.11 Sunny weather and shallow riffles reduce anxious feelings about wading.

Wading and Safety

In guiding classes of beginning anglers, I have found that many people who are unaccustomed to walking in trout streams become quite anxious about their safety. Actually feeling the current against their legs does little to reassure them, and often distracts them from the attention needed in learning to fish. Consequently, I prefer to give my basic fly fishing instruction where currents don't move fast enough to be disconcerting, and under sunny conditions when the stream bottom is clearly visible.

An additional advantage of selecting the warm part of the day to fish is evident if you are unable to purchase hip or chest waders. The warm conditions enable you to "wade wet" in relative comfort. You may even find you prefer to wade in wet jeans when temperatures permit. However, you should be aware that it could lead to hypothermia if practiced in cold conditions or if you delay changing your wet clothes after fishing.

If there is a cardinal rule of safety while wading it is to wade well within your limits. These limits can be extended through experience or through the assistance of a good instructor.

Riffles are generally safe places to wade. In them you typically fish from the shallow, gently sloping side of the stream where small, gravel-sized rocks have been deposited. However, movements toward deeper water may lead you to areas where the stream bottom slopes more abruptly. Here some danger exists because gravel on a slope can move underfoot and create a ball-bearing effect that can slide you to a dunking in deep water.

Variations of This Method

The downstream drift and across-stream swing of a fly forms the basis for several other more specific and demanding fly fishing methods. For example, by casting a longer line, developing distinctive retrieves, and roll casting a sinking line to the surface, you have the essentials of big river streamer (i.e., a fly that imitates a bait fish) fishing and steelhead fishing. E.H. "Polly" Rosborough, the highly regarded nymph tyer and angler, has found a down-and-across approach well suited to his shallow nymph and streamer techniques on the wide, moderately paced rivers he fishes in southern Oregon.

The down-and-across wet fly technique I most enjoy came to me from still water expert Hal Janssen, and involves wide meadow streams, slow-sinking lines, and a fly that imitates a leech. Here the cast is made directly across stream or just slightly upstream. The problem with casting more directly upstream is that some of the sinking line will drift downstream ahead of the fly and cause it to swing across the water unrealistically fast as the line straightens below you. So you cast across stream and, as the line sinks, you shake out a little more line through the guides of the fly rod (a technique described in chapter 9). Then you mend the line often enough to keep it entirely upstream of the fly. As the fly finally makes its slow swing across the stream, you may want to retrieve in short strips of line. You hope to impart a slight up-and-down rocking motion to the fly, suggestive of the movement of a swimming leech.

Selected Readings

Borger, G. (1979, July/August). Invertebrate drift. *Rod and Reel*.

Hidy, V. (1961). *Sports Illustrated book of wet–fly fishing*. Philadelphia: Lippincott.

Leisenring, J., & Hidy, V. (1971). *The art of tying the wet fly and fishing the nymph*. New York: Crown.

Nemes, S. (1975). *The soft hackled fly*. Old Greenwich, CT: Chatham.

Rosborough, E.H. (1978). *Tying and fishing the fuzzy nymphs*. Harrisburg, PA: Stackpole.

3
Chapter

Dry Fly Fishing in Mountain Lakes: A Basic Lake Method

*I*f you are ready to learn dry (floating) fly fishing, try to locate a lake where trout feed hungrily on the surface. Many alpine lakes are ideal for learning this method because their unusually short growing season and sterile water force trout to feed almost constantly, inhaling anything that swims, crawls, or flies too close. Often one or two trout will cruise in a straight path just off shore trying to obtain enough food to survive.

This cruising behavior illustrates a basic distinction between lake-dwelling and stream-dwelling trout. Trout in lakes most often cruise or move to find food, whereas trout in streams tend to hold in or move to feeding stations and take food carried within reach by the current.

Dry fly fishing is easier to learn in a mountain lake than in a stream because the line handling in the lake method is simpler. When you first attempt to float an artificial fly, there is enough to think about in keeping it visible, remaining alert for rises, and

Figure 3.1   Hollow deer hair and stiff hackle contribute to the flotation that keeps the Horner Deer Hair (Humpy) visible on riffled surfaces.

setting the hook properly, without also having to make sure you are stripping line in to coincide with an ever-changing current.

Seeing a wild trout rise to a surface fly provides the excitement that keeps some people fishing exclusively with dry flies throughout their lives.

Rigging Adaptations

Our general-purpose fly rod and line are well suited to this method of fly fishing, though lake anglers don't always agree on the type of floating line to use. If you fish where trees or high rock ledges prevent a back cast, you may prefer the roll-casting (discussed in this chapter) capability of a double-tapered line. However, if obstacles to casting are not a problem and you are experienced in casting with a double haul (discussed in chapter 6), you will most likely prefer the distance advantages of a weight-forward line.

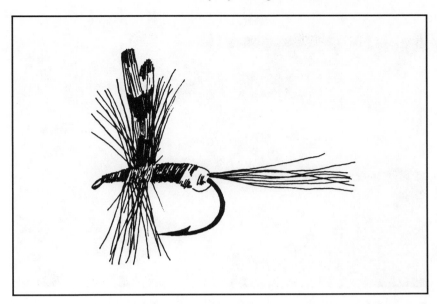

Figure 3.2   The ever-present Adams is our most popular "standard dry fly" for quiet water. The light body color near the tail of this one represents a mayfly's egg sac.

Fish are often spooky in clear lake water, so our 9-foot leader may need to be lengthened to 12 feet at times. Under these conditions you may want to switch from a typical, general-purpose "attractor" dry fly, such as a size 12 Horner Deer Hair (Humpy), to a smaller and more delicate pattern, such as a size 14 or 16 Adams. While the Humpy is constructed to float on more turbulent water than the Adams, both are superb general-purpose flies: Both are tied with mixed brown and grizzly hackle (i.e., the feather wrapped around the hook to represent the legs and sometimes the wings of an insect) and are medium-toned to cover the widest spectrum of colors commonly seen in aquatic insects. Also both patterns have general insect shapes that take fish when either caddisflies or mayflies are on the water or when nothing at all is on the water. Whichever fly you select should feature stiff hackle and tail material to help keep it floating as intended.

I recall a few moments on Lake Solitude in Grand Teton National Park when this basic mountain-lake rigging served me

Figure 3.3   Keep low to avoid being seen by cruising trout in transparent water.

well. The 15-mile round-trip hike was taking longer than my wife Barbara and I had anticipated, so we had agreed to stop at the lake only long enough to eat lunch. But coming up the trail I had assembled my rod and attached a size 14 Adams to the 9-foot leader (backpacking anglers learn to assemble equipment on the move). As I ate, the rod was at my side with 35 feet of line on the ground beyond the rod tip. No one we had met on the trail that day had seen a fish rise, but as luck would have it, one rose while I was eating—within casting range. I laid down my sandwich, picked up the fly rod, and caught a 14-inch cutthroat on one cast, without even getting up. Trout are seldom so accommodating.

The Approach

Perhaps the most fundamental principle in approaching a trout lake or stream is that the quieter and clearer the water, the more careful and stealthy must be your approach. Thus in clear alpine lakes, it may be necessary to use a tree or a rock as a

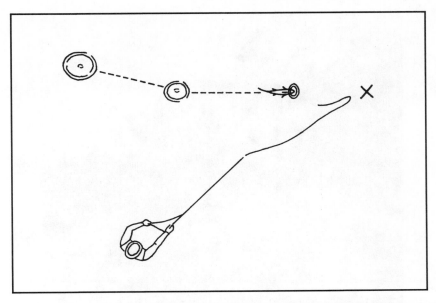

Figure 3.4   Casting beyond the second rise is based on the trout's tendency to cruise in a relatively straight line.

"blind" and then to cast the fly well ahead of any visible fish so they will not be spooked by the cast. More typically, however, you will try to analyze the pattern of rises (i.e., the trout's surface feeding). If a cruising fish rises frequently, you learn to wait for its second rise to determine the direction the trout is moving, and then place the fly ahead of it. When rises are isolated and fish are not too spooky, you cast directly to the spot of the rise. To get it there soon enough, you may have to be false casting so that your line is already in the air when a promising rise appears.

At times the fish in such lakes are not rising but may still be taken on a dry fly. Under these conditions, you should be playing the percentages in locating fish rather than casting randomly along some shoreline. Move to a spot where you believe fish are likely to be found. One such spot would be the outlet of a lake, where currents converge and carry surface food from a wide area into the same spot. Another high-percentage spot for locating trout is near the inlet where fresh, oxygenated water and some food enter the lake. Fishing near aquatic vegetation is also worthwhile because it provides cover for trout as well as cover and

Figure 3.5   In the roll cast you draw the line back on the water rather than cast it back in the air.

food for the aquatic animals trout feed on. Partially submerged rocks or logs near shore also provide shaded cover in the vicinity of land insects, such as ants and beetles, that are frequently blown into lakes.

Casting Techniques

In dry fly fishing, the false cast helps to dry your fly off for the next presentation. Casting is normally done with the basic

Figure 3.6   A late power application drives the line out efficiently in a low oval roll.

overhead cast, though the roll cast becomes an important tool on lakes where trees crowd the shoreline and prevent back casting.

The roll cast starts when the line has been slowly drawn back toward you on the water and the rod tip is back just past vertical. The elbow of your casting arm may be at least as high as your shoulder at the start of the forward stroke to provide more distance through which your hand can move down in applying power. The maximum acceleration comes when the rod tip is forward enough to provide a low, knifing oval in the line's roll-out. The "circle shaped" roll sometimes pictured doesn't have the same distance potential and usually results from applying power too early in the cast. This is an important teaching point in Mel Krieger's instruction.

Several variations of the basic cast are useful in lake fly fishing. The ability to "shoot line" enables you to add distance to your cast. To do this, simply strip extra line off the reel and let it slip through the fingers of your line hand (and out through the guides

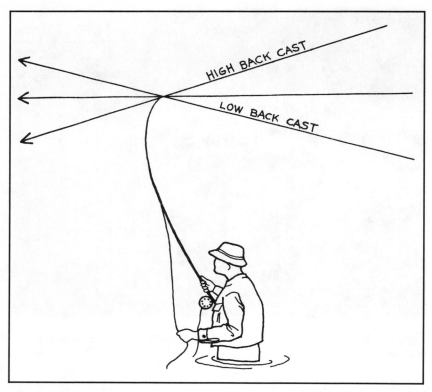

Figure 3.7   Casting from low back cast to high forward cast carries the fly when the wind comes from behind. High back cast to low forward cast drives the fly line into a wind that blows into your face.

of your rod) on the forward cast. If the line doesn't shoot, you are most likely letting it go too early in the forward cast. When students have this problem, I advise them to release with the line hand only when they can see the loop form in the line in front of them. Certainly shooting line works better with a weight-forward line than with a double-tapered line.

Wind often comes up on lakes so you may have to make adjustments in the basic cast. To use a wind from behind to your advantage, you lower the angle of your back cast and raise that of your forward cast; in this way the wind carries your fly farther. A wind into your face can be overcome by raising your back cast and lowering the forward cast to get a low, hard-driving layout of line.

Figure 3.8   Dropping your fly into the circle made by a trout's rise brings anticipation and excitement.

A wind blowing toward your casting arm from the side prompts you to move the fly line and hook over to the protected, noncasting side of your body. You do this by canting your rod tip over to that side and executing the off-side cast described in chapter 10.

Line-Handling and Fishing Techniques

In most dry fly fishing in lakes, you permit the fly to drift naturally on the surface without being twitched. The only line-handling is an occasional stripping-in of slack that forms as a result of wave action. This line-handling is much easier than that needed to continually keep pace with the currents of most streams.

A trout that is approaching your fly should not be able to see you. Crouching and keeping a low silhouette will help. But when your fly begins to drift close enough for fish and fisherman to see each other, the fly should be lifted gently off the water and recast to a spot farther away. If no fish are rising, you may want to cover the water systematically by casting to various angles with a relatively short cast and then "fanning" across again with longer casts. This is nothing more than a lake variation of the near-to-far concept.

Hooking and Landing the Fish

Playing a small trout in a mountain lake provides the opportunity to practice techniques that will help you to land the next large trout that in a single moment picks up your fly and numbs your senses. The clarity of such lakes permits you to observe the fish being played, including what happens when you add pressure by bending your fly rod. One thing you learn is to make your pressure adjustments in response to the direction the trout is facing. For example, if the trout is already contributing to its own exhaustion by moving away from you, don't put additional tension on your tippet by bending the rod forcefully. You should also go easy with the rod while a fish is moving toward you. In that case, undue tension on the line could pull the fly out of the trout's mouth. All that's needed is to minimize slack line by stripping or reeling it in. The time to bend your rod is when the fish faces sideways to you; then you can pull it off balance or disorient it and thus force it to keep expending energy. My friend, Bob Dering, and I thought up the following mnemonic for this fish-playing distinction: "Head in or away, let the fish play. Head left or right, pull up tight."

Putting pressure on the fish at the right time is an important conservation measure that is often overlooked by many otherwise capable fly fishermen. This tactic enables you to get the fish in and release it faster, which increases its chances for survival.

I have my students practice these movements on the casting field by playing a "human fish." Bob Giannoni, the former head master of the Fenwick School at West Yellowstone, gave me this drill to which I have added other adjustments, such as lowering the rod tip and "bowing to the fish" when the "fish" jumps. This drill is really fun for the person playing the trout's role, creates some realistic panic in the angler, and most importantly helps prepare students for handling a strong fish.

Wading and Safety

Some backpackers who fly fish the high mountain lakes leave their waders at home. They find it difficult to justify space for such a large item. Instead of wading, they often fish when the trout have moved in toward shore—during morning and evening hours.

Other backpackers don extra pants and tennis shoes, choosing to wade wet. Care must be taken to respect the danger of hypothermia from the combination of cold lake water and fast-cooling afternoons.

Among the most dedicated fly fishing backpackers are a group who insist on taking along a pair of modern, lightweight, stocking-foot waders to use with tennis shoes. A few even pack in light-weight inflatable float tubes so that they can cover all the water.

Variations of This Method

The trout in lakes often become selective in their surface feeding, which leads you into the world of "matching the hatch," that is, obtaining fly patterns that are specific imitations of the insects fish are feeding on (discussed in chapter 12). Mayflies and midges are two common sources of this selective feeding.

At times you will find that a naturally drifting fly isn't as effective in attracting trout as one that is actively manipulated. On such occasions you intentionally create motion by twitching, skittering, or crawling your fly to excite the trout. If you see ants struggling in the surface film, caddisflies paddling toward shore while emerging, or winged insects skittering along the surface while depositing their eggs, you have a behavior to imitate when retrieving your fly.

Sometimes trout feed on insects floating or moving just under the surface. You should consider this possibility when only the trout's back breaks the surface during its rise. When you see this, change your fly to something such as an unweighted nymph or a spinner pattern (i.e., dying adult mayfly), fished flush in the surface film or slightly submerged.

Selected Readings

Almy, G. (1981, Winter). What makes a good dry fly. *The flyfisher*.

Cordes, R., & Kaufmann, R. (1984). *Lake fishing with a fly*. Portland, OR: Frank Amato.

Mitchell, R. (1981, Early Spring). Recommendation for an alpine idyll. *Angler*.

Rajeff, S. (1977, January/February). Casting with Steve Rajeff—The roll cast. *Angler*.

Raymond, S. (1977). Still water—Ponds and lakes. In J. Migel (Ed.), *The masters on the dry fly*. Philadelphia: Lippincott.

Roberts, D. (1978, March/April). Lakes: Scratching the surface. *Flyfishing the west*.

Shaw, J. (1980). *Fly fish the trout lakes*. Mitchell Press.

Chapter *4*

Short-Line, Dry Fly Fishing: A First Upstream Presentation

*T*he water type that is most appropriate to the method discussed here is "pocket water"—short pools of slow water found among the faster currents of mountain streams. These short pools may be formed by large rocks, logs, or other obstacles that deflect the stream's currents, either at midstream or along a bank. Such "pocket water" is typical of the steeper sections of small mountain streams or of the cascading runs of large streams. When a big midstream rock diverts current flow, it creates small areas of slower moving water that provide a mini-environment where aquatic plants flourish, slow-water insects colonize, and trout hold without expending much energy. For dry fly fishing, shallow pockets are generally best because bottom-holding trout will often move the two or three feet to the surface; the deeper the pocket water, the less likely the bigger fish will rise to feed on top.

Dry flies work well throughout long periods of the day in many creeks. This is partly because food is seldom abundant there, and trout become accustomed to rising to any terrestrial insects that happen to fall onto the water. In narrow creeks it is not unrealistic to think of trout as the ultimate "bank feeders,"

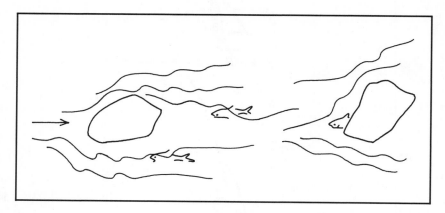

Figure 4.1 In rock-strewn water, trout often hold along the edges between fast and slow currents.

because both banks contribute food to the same fish. In alpine creeks the winter kill of insects and the sterility of water add to a trout's survival problems and lead to almost continual feeding.

The problems you face in fishing pocket water are largely a result of the short length of pools or the extreme variation in current speed. These factors should prompt you to move in close to the fish in order to keep your fly from being dragged along the surface by currents moving at different speeds. The most common error I notice among quiet-water flyrodders who attempt to fish pocket water is the tendency to fish too much line. Fishing a short line is one of the ways to minimize the buildup of slack in an upstream-cast line.

Rigging Adaptations

Our basic fly rod, reel, and line will work well in pocket water, though many anglers who fish regularly in such water prefer a rod action with some flex into the butt of the rod so it will bend enough to present a fly delicately when only a few feet of fly line extend beyond the rod tip. Stiffness in a rod butt often makes an important, positive contribution to loop control where long casts are used, but it interferes with the feel I prefer when casting a short

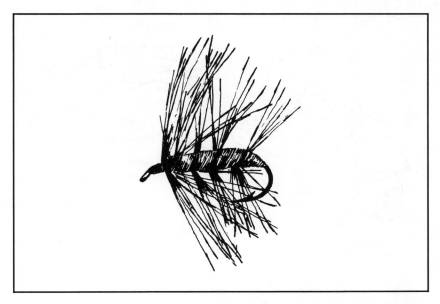

Figure 4.2 Wrapping the hackle the length of a fly's body is called palmering. In this Orange Palmer the over-sized hackle contributes to the fly's enticing fluttery drift in mixed currents, which creates an impression of the wing-flapping behavior of egg-laying caddisflies and stoneflies.

line in pocket water. One way to pick up more feel throughout your rod is to fish it with a slightly heavier line than the manufacturer recommends.

Also related to these short casts is the use of short leaders, typically from 6 to 7-1/2 feet in length. Short leaders enable you to let out a little additional line beyond the rod tip to load the rod when casting at close range. It is easier to cast line than leader.

Most pocket-water dry fly anglers have one or two favorite general-purpose fly patterns, usually in sizes 10 or 12. The moderate degree of surface turbulence often makes it difficult to see smaller flies, and the ability to see the fly is necessary to hook a high percentage of the fish that take. Some anglers drop down to a size 14 fly during the day, when visibility is good, and work back up to a size 10 at dusk. A buoyant, general-purpose fly, such as a Horner Deer Hair (i.e., Goofus Bug, Humpy), is usually a better choice in this type of water than one that imitates a particular insect.

Figure 4.3   Pocket-water dry fly anglers must often change position to keep fly, leader, and line on the same drift lane.

My favorite dry fly for this type of fishing is an old standard in northern California, a size 10 Orange Palmer. This fly is known elsewhere as the Palmer Sedge or Orange Asher; it is a life-like imitation of egg-laying caddisflies and stoneflies. The long, stiff hackles wound the length of the hook shank not only help keep the fly up, but provide air resistance during the cast. This enables you to drop the fly gently, when using an unusually short leader. Other patterns, such as Bi-visibles, Variants, and Spiders, share this feature and are effective in pocket water.

The Approach

In short-line methods where you must get close to the fish, the approach to the hole is very important. Trout, which face upcurrent to be able to see food drifting down toward them, are much more likely to see you when you wade down the stream than when you wade upstream from behind them.

Figure 4.4 Casting upstream and keeping low gets you close enough to present the fly where mixed currents prevent long drifts.

But concealment from the trout includes more than approaching from behind. It also means keeping low, whether by submerging part of your body in wading, crouching low, dropping to one knee, or even crawling on your stomach. If a trout can see you as it turns upward toward the fly, or swims downstream in pursuit of the fly, you aren't low enough. Some anglers become so experienced at knowing how much a trout can see in a particular spot that they will save energy by hunching over only after their cast and only as much as necessary.

Casting position is determined not only by the need for concealment, but also by the need to achieve a "natural" drift of the fly—as if there were no leader attached to it. As a dry fly angler, the more you cast across the stream, the more the line and leader fall on currents that move at different speeds. If part of the line or leader gets ahead of the fly, it will pull the fly across stream, producing "drag." In order to prevent drag in mixed currents, you should attempt to get the fly, leader, and line to fall in the same drift lane so they all move at roughly the same speed. This

Figure 4.5   Adjusting to close targets with a long rod means tilting the casting plane forward—lowering forward casts and raising back casts.

means finding a casting position that permits you a cast aimed straight upstream or nearly so. The turbulence of surface currents in pocket water is often sufficient to conceal your leader from trout beneath it.

So the approach used here is quite different from that described for fishing the downstream angles of a wide riffle (chapter 2). Here you buck the current, position yourself more precisely, and cast to "targets" unlike the systematic covering of one large run.

Casting Techniques

The angler who fishes short pools seems to be flicking line back and forth constantly, without any noticeable pause between back cast and forward cast. This fast-casting rhythm is due primarily to two things: first, it takes almost no time to straighten 10 to 15 feet of line behind the rod, and second, some of the pools are so short that long drifts are impossible and so turbulent that

Figure 4.6 Should the fly land first? In the short pool on top, the fly should land when the leader does to be on the water for the full length of the drift. In the long, slow riffle below, a gentle drop of the fly often occurs after some line and leader have touched down.

repeated drifts are necessary to make sure the trout have seen the fly.

Pin-point accuracy in casting is often important in this fishing. George Dozier had an interesting way of teaching his 11-year-old pupil this lesson. He would often invite me to make the first casts into particularly promising pools. When I would fail to raise a fish, he would shake his head as if he couldn't understand why a fish hadn't risen and then cast an identical pattern into what I thought was the same spot. Only this time a trout would rise to take the fly. The first few times this happened, I attributed it to my bad luck. But when it kept happening, I found myself beginning to notice differences in exactly where our flies were landing. Only then did I take fish. As an initial guideline, you want to place your fly in a drift lane that moves it between about 6 and 12 inches a second.

There are at least two adjustments you can make to your basic cast for effective short-line dry fly fishing. One is to tilt the casting plane forward. The longer your fly rod, the more pronounced

Figure 4.7   Splitting concentration here refers to the need to watch the line to keep it lifted off fast water as well as the need to watch the drifting fly.

the forward tilt must be to drop the fly as close as 20 feet away. Lowering the plane of your forward cast to reach such nearby targets means that you must elevate your back cast, if you are to maintain the 180 degree separation between a straightened line behind you and a straightened line in front.

A second basic adjustment may be necessary when you have to present the fly under overhanging branches. Here you learn to cant or tilt the fly rod down to one side (the right side for a right handed caster) to make a sidearm cast. In doing this, your casting forearm is also canted to coincide with the angle of the fly rod. If necessary, you can also lower your right hip as a means of lowering the angle of the fly rod even farther. The line should unroll on the cast to form loops in a horizontal plane.

Eventually you become proficient in using the fly rod in various casting angles— sidearm, three-quarters overhead, almost vertical, and even tipped to the left side.

The presence of streamside foliage also teaches you to look back before casting. A slight change in the angle of the back cast may keep the fly from hanging up in a tree. At times the foliage is so thick that a back cast is impossible, and the roll cast (discussed in the previous chapter) or some short-line flip of the rod becomes necessary to present the fly. If you do hook up in a tree, don't feel bad; it happens to the most famous fly fishermen in the world.

Line-Handling and Fishing Techniques

Frequently line-handling begins with the cast itself. When fishing short pools, your fly should land at about the same time the leader and line do. If the fly lands first, it may sink because nothing else has first absorbed the shock of landing on the water. If, however, your line and leader land much before the fly, they are drifting toward the fast water at the tail of the pool while the fly is still airborne—with the result that some of the fishable drift is lost. And the drifts are short enough already in pocket water.

One of the most difficult things about fishing a dry fly in short pools is that your concentration must be divided. On the one hand, you need to watch the fly itself for the earliest indication of a rising trout. But on the other hand you must watch the line at the point where it leaves the water. If part of the line is allowed to drift into the faster water at the tail of the pool where it tumbles into the next one, the line immediately picks up speed, pulls on the fly, and ruins the natural drift.

So it is important in this method, and in any upstream fly fishing method, to gather in line at the same speed the current brings it down to you. It is this element more than any other that makes upstream fly fishing more difficult initially than the two methods already described. The ability to strip in line fast enough to prevent the buildup of slack takes practice but is essential to setting the hook before the trout has had time to spit it out. I provide this practice for my students when they are first attempting dry fly technique on the stream. As the fly begins to drift after the cast, I call "strike" to test how quickly and effectively they can set the hook. They get the idea very quickly that line control is as important as casting is to hooking fish.

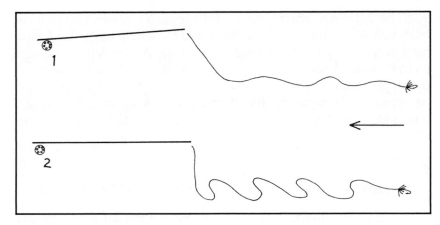

Figure 4.8 An upstream-cast line must be gathered in fast enough to prevent the formation of slack. An angler holding the rod on top (1) can set the hook into a rising fish with a short, precise movement of the rod and line, whereas such precision is difficult for an angler holding the other rod (2).

Though some anglers gather in line by means of the technique called the "hand twist" retrieve, I teach stripping in line because it is easier for beginners to learn and more versatile.

Many students ask how high to hold their rod tip when fishing this type of water. Although I prefer to fish with a low rod tip whenever possible (particularly in windy conditions), I find here that my tip is often up as high as necessary to keep my leader or line from falling onto fast currents. I feel it's important to do whatever I can to maintain a slow drift of the fly. I have watched my skilled friend, Frank Collin, fish dry flies on certain turbulent sections of California's Truckee River with his fly rod held high and almost vertical. He does so when he is fishing slots of slow water so narrow that there is room for only his fly and a foot or so of tippet. Though anything but an ideal rod position for setting the hook, this is the only rod position that will bring the fish to the fly in the first place in such water. While only some of these fish reach the net, all provide excitement.

One of the basic fishing concepts that has been handed down from one generation of flyrodders to the next asserts that the first cast to a pool is the one most likely to catch fish and that your chances diminish with each successive cast. This concept

Figure 4.9   The small patch of dark water between the two rocks on the right is best fished by "dapping the fly." Pulsating hackles of flies dapped on the surface sometimes bring fish up from cover when nothing else will.

generally holds true in small streams or pocket water when fish are hungry. When trout are inactive, however, it sometimes pays off to work a good spot thoroughly, as repeated casts seem to induce strikes from some trout.

Whenever trout begin to feed actively, the experienced angler is quick to sense the change in the stream's biology and adjust to it by moving upstream faster and making fewer casts to each pool. The underlying principle becomes one of fishing over as many hungry fish as possible during the "hot" period. In larger streams, where many fish occupy the same run, it may be better to move to the best holding water in that stretch and remain there.

There is a tendency for some beginners to want to remove the fly from the water if it has been poorly cast. This is usually a mistake, because even large fish can be taken on sloppy casts.

Trout are not casting critics. However, there is a time when I will lift my fly off early in the drift—when it starts to sink from my view. In this kind of fishing, you strive to keep the fly visible in rough water. If it begins to sink, the fly is absorbing water which will spoil its flotation in subsequent drifts. Also a submerged fly is not visible in some light conditions, causing strikes to be missed that wouldn't be if the fly were visible.

The visibility of the fly is so important that pocket water anglers are forever doing things to dry it off, including false casting, re-applying flotants, absorbing the moisture in chamois-like cloths or commercial powders, changing flies, and even intentionally casting to hit a rock, so the fly will bounce off and land gently on the water. Snagging your fly in a tree will dry it off, too—if you can get the fly back.

Hooking and Landing the Fish

If you fail to hook rising trout it can be for several reasons. A trout that suddenly turns and bolts away has probably seen you, indicating inadequate concealment. If the trout spits out the fly before the hook is set, either you weren't watching the fly or permitted excessive slack to form in the line on the water. Any time you set the hook at what seems to be the right moment, and the fish isn't hooked, you should develop the habit of checking to make sure the point isn't broken. The failure to do this may cost you other fish that day.

I learned this lesson the hard way. It was mid-June and a foot of snow covered the banks of little Foster Creek, 8,000 feet high in the Sierra. I could tell from where the footprints were positioned in the snow that the angler ahead of me was experienced and left-handed (as I am). That angler left me little: Only three fish rose to my fly that afternoon. It surprised me when I missed the first two, because the takes had been deliberate. I knew my timing was perfect on the third miss, but only then did I check and find the broken hook. It's interesting how well we learn when forced to walk home skunked.

If the small trout you hook come flying back toward you in the air, you have set with too much force. Such force will often break the tippet when larger fish are hooked. The hook should be set as gently as possible, and fish "played" back toward you under water by stripping in line. It is not necessary to reel in the slack line and "play the fish off the reel" unless you have hooked a large trout.

Wading and Safety

Many anglers learn their basic wading skills and thus develop confidence while fishing small streams, where the current force is not excessive and slips are seldom hazardous. The wading becomes essential to reach some of the best fish, whether in brush-lined brooks or midstream pockets of wide rivers.

Even in small, gentle streams, anglers soon learn to glue either felt or Ozite indoor-outdoor carpeting to the soles of their wading footgear to minimize slipping on smooth or algae-covered rocks.

Don't let yourself be tempted to hop from one dry rock to another on shallow streams. This is a dangerous practice because dry rocks can be slippery, and you could hit your head and drown in shallow water. Even dry, apparently safe footing should be tested before weight is fully transferred, particularly in the vicinity of a stream.

This is also true of logs, which can be quite slippery. Log jams often provide the shortest route between point A and point B on those obstacle courses known as trout streams. However, insecure footing or rotting wood can cause you to fall through such jams and risk serious injury.

Variations of This Method

Many small streams have sections that are overgrown with alders or other moisture-loving, low-growing trees. Quite often these sections contain more and bigger trout than do accessible stretches and offer the opportunity of action well into the season as well as an escape from anglers who intrude on your solitude.

To catch fish in such places requires fighting through brush, crawling on hands and knees, and resorting to a no-cast, short-line version of dapping, where a foot or so of a very short leader may be all that drops from a rod tip poked between alder branches. It is not fly fishing as popularly conceived, but it can be great fun and quite instructive to anyone new to the sport.

Once the basics of this short-line, dry fly method are learned, it should not be difficult for you to make a transition to longer casts and longer pools in your dry fly fishing. This subject is covered in chapter 8.

Selected Readings

Betters, F. (1981, Mid–Season). Picking pockets. *Fly Fisherman*.

Flick, A. (1977). How to fish pocket water. In J. Migel (Ed.), *The masters of the dry fly*. Philadelphia: Lippincott.

Humphreys, J. (1984, September). Conquering lip currents. *Fly Fisherman*.

McClane, A.J. (1974, January). The dry fly on fast water. *Field & Stream*.

McClane, A.J. (1974, September). All-hackle—The valuable tackle.

Big Fly Nymphing in Big Streams: Adapting to Increased Current Speed and Depth

*T*he combined current speed and depth of some trout water, whether in the form of wide, choppy riffles or fast, smooth-topped glides, is sufficient to create a problem in getting your fly down to the bottom in time to attract fish. So distinctive adaptations must be made to the basic down-and-across sunken-fly method (described in chapter 2) if you are to fish effectively in such big water.

Trout in fast, deep runs are often large and generally hold where a big rock or a depression on the stream's bottom has created a niche of slow water. These "bottom pockets" are seldom visible from above the water's surface, and the fast surrounding currents tend to keep the fish close to home in their feeding. So we have "pockets" we can't see containing fish that don't move. The implication is to use a systematic method that provides a thorough coverage of the stream's bottom.

I remember a particular bottom pocket that "Polly" Rosborough alerted me to on the Williamson River in Oregon. As he described

Figure 5.1   Fast, deep runs present a unique set of problems for the nymphing angler.

a pool he wanted me to try, he cautioned me that the biggest fish would be holding below an obvious boil on the water's surface. He said the boil and the depression the fish would be holding in were both formed by a large submerged rock. For some reason I didn't get to that pool until the next summer. My friend Dick Holland reached the water first, looked it over, and moved up to the head of the pool. When I arrived, I agreed that Dick had selected the best looking water, but I moved toward the tail of the pool to find Polly's boil. It turned out that Dick's water produced a feisty 14-inch rainbow, just seven inches shorter than the one I found. So my appreciation for bottom pockets and for a man known affectionately as "Polly" grew that day. And don't feel sorry for Dick; he took a four-and-a-half pound rainbow earlier that morning.

Rigging Adaptations

Our basic fly rod will catch fish with this method, but if you

Figure 5.2 "Bottom pockets" or depressions may be formed by ledges or large, submerged rocks.

fish such water regularly, you will use a rod that does a better job of casting heavy flies. This latter rod typically takes a number 7 or 8 fly line, is 8-1/2 to 9 feet long, and is stiffer through the whole rod, particularly throughout the tip section, than normal.

The floating fly line will often be replaced by one designed to sink. The faster and deeper the water, the greater is the need for a sinking line. A fast-sinking line will be most useful, though serious anglers often have several different types to be able to vary the sink rate when fishing different runs. Where casting distance is required to cover the far reaches of a heavy riffle, shooting-taper fly lines may be preferred. These short 30-foot fly lines can either be purchased or fashioned by cutting that length off one end of a full-length, double-tapered fly line.

Leaders used with these sinking lines are typically short, between four and six feet in length. With so little distance between the fly and fly line, the sinking qualities of each combine to overcome any buoyancy in the leader. Longer leaders will keep the fly from sinking to bottom levels as quickly as you would like.

Leader tippet diameters may be .009 inch (2X) or larger as required to turn over a heavily weighted fly in the cast as well as to hold big fish that use their weight and the force of the current against you when hooked.

The flies selected for such fast, heavy water are almost always big (e.g., sizes 2–8) and heavily weighted (e.g., hook shank wrapped with 2–5 amp lead fuse wire). A fly should be big enough

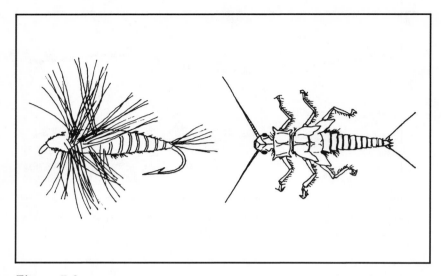

Figure 5.3   Large meals are associated with trout in big, turbulent water. Heavily weighted flies, such as the Brook's Montana Stone, resemble fast-water stonefly nymphs in size, shape, and color.

to attract the trout's attention in turbulent flow as well as to represent the mouthful of food it needs to replace the energy expended in chasing its prey through currents. Also a big fly allows you to add more weight to the shank of the hook than is possible with a smaller one of the same design. Coincidentally, the bottoms of these fast runs harbor large insects, crustaceans, and forage fish so the large flies also simulate existing prey.

Another feature of the fly that is considered important is that it appear to be alive. One way to achieve this impression of life in a fly that is drifting downstream (rather than being jerked or moved across the current) is to use materials that will pulsate in the currents. Hackles tied along the shank of big flies do a good job of this and conceal the fact that some of these flies look like nothing that ever lived.

I would guess that the big fly most commonly used in deep, fast runs is a weighted Woolly-Worm, with a black or brown body, tied on a size 4 or 6 hook. While the Woolly-Worm is a generalist pattern, many knowledgeable anglers select fly patterns that more closely resemble the most abundant, large foods in such water: big stoneflies or sculpins.

The Approach

Stealth is less important in this kind of fly fishing than in any other. The turbulence of heavy, fast water and the bottom-holding tendencies of the fish permit you to make an approach from up and across stream. This is fortunate because an upstream-cast fly in fast water moves downstream past you so quickly that downstream fishing angles are required to achieve a sufficiently long drift to attract fish.

As in the basic down-and-across swing, the typical progression is to fish from the head of the pool to the tail, stopping every few steps to cover the water from near to far. A long run of a good-sized river will take an hour or more to fish with such thorough coverage.

Casting Techniques

Although the fishing occurs downstream of you, casts are quartered up and across the stream in this method. The combined depth and current speed require an upstream cast, the purpose of which is to provide time for the fly to reach the bottom while still upstream of the trout. Although the cast is angled upstream, your feet should be planted to face down and across stream—the direction you will be facing when the fly reaches the fish.

The cast should be made with a large, open loop to keep the heavily weighted fly away from your head. My teaching requirement that students wear a hat and sunglasses to protect the head and eyes becomes particularly important when casting heavy flies.

A casting variation sometimes referred to as a "tension cast" becomes useful in covering the far side of wide riffles. The tension is created by allowing the weighted terminal tackle (i.e., weight on leader and/or fly) to trail just under the surface once the line has straightened downstream at the completion of the drift. Then, when power is applied smoothly in the forward cast, this tension bends the rod. As the line comes off the water and the cast is completed, the fly is propelled a considerable distance up and across stream. The best description of this cast I know of can be found in Charles Brooks' book, *Nymph Fishing for Larger Trout* (1976, p. 128).

Figure 5.4   A large, open loop is cast when you need to keep a weighted
leader away from your head.

Line-Handling and Fishing Techniques

After the upstream cast, the fly sinks and drifts through water
that was already fished from farther upstream. So don't expect
strikes until the fly has drifted opposite you or some distance
downstream of your position. But you should already be doing
some line-handling as the fly is drifting down toward you. If you
fail to do so, slack will form in the line under water with the result
that too many strikes will go undetected. Some inexperienced flyrodders attempt to minimize this problem by stripping in line as
it approaches them from above, and then are faced with another

Figure 5.5 Casting upstream (to the right) provides time for a fly to sink before being fished in the heavy riffle off to the angler's left. The dark rock under the caster's arm serves as a reference point for this series of three photos.

problem of feeding line out again as the fly moves away downstream. Otherwise they don't have enough line out to reach the trout below.

A better way to solve this problem is to lift the line off the water as it comes toward you from upstream by raising the fly rod and arms as much as necessary. The line that would be forming slack under water is lifted off, but not stripped in. Then as the fly moves away from you downstream, this line becomes available again as you lower the rod and arms and lay the line back on the water as straight as possible. All this while, the fly has had time to sink to the bottom. In my opinion, the development and popularization of this rod-handling technique is Charles Brooks' most important contribution to fly fishing.

Strikes may come during the ensuing drift or when the fly swings across stream below you. The retrieve or next cast should be delayed for several seconds until the fly has had time to catch up with the line.

So in this method, you first try to get the fly deep, then allow it to tumble freely or "dead drift" for a distance, until the line

Figure 5.6 Raising the fly rod and arms ''a la Brooks'' keeps extra line off the water when the fly is closest to you.

tightens and swings the fly across the current toward you. The fly may be activated as you retrieve for the next cast. However, many anglers also impart some sort of action to the fly throughout the drift, at least at times. Where the water moves slowly enough that the submerged line remains fairly straight, I tend to activate my fly either by stripping with the line hand or giving my rod tip little upstream jerks. I usually strip in line because it gives me a more constant feel to the fly, but will use the rod tip instead when I want to fish all the fly line I have cast throughout the drift. When the current is fast enough to put a bend in the

Figure 5.7   When the fly is downstream and the line is lowered again, you are ready to begin fishing.

submerged line, I typically use both hands together in much the same way that I sometimes set the hook. I pull back upstream with the rod enough to straighten as much of the line as I can and simultaneously strip in enough line to move the fly slightly.

Hooking and Landing Techniques

If you frequent heavy waters and use big-fly methods, you soon learn to keep your hooks sharpened for the quickest penetration of hook points. The strong tippets permit you to set the hook vigorously. I often set the hook twice in this type of fishing to make sure the big hook has penetrated sufficiently. Large trout hooked downstream of you often move farther in that direction and gain a considerable headstart. Frequently it becomes necessary to wade ashore and get downstream of the fish so that when it moves away from you it must fight the current as well as your fly rod.

The decision of whether to play the fish from midstream or wade ashore is not always easy to make. It involves a quick analy-

Figure 5.8 Submerge the net before bringing the fish toward you. Avoid sudden swiping or reaching motions that could further alarm a half-exhausted trout.

Figure 5.9 Soon to be released, this trout should be handled gently. Injury could result from its entanglement in the mesh.

Figure 5.10   Metal-bottomed footwear, such as the Stream Cleat being held here and the Boot Chain on the other foot, offers more protection against slipping in streams than does felt alone.

sis of the amount of line the fish has taken out, the type of water the fish is moving through, and the toughness of the wade.

Should you decide to net the fish in midstream, it is important to develop the habit of lifting with the net, rather than reaching or swiping with it. The net is placed under water, the fish is maneuvered over it, and then the net is lifted.

Choose a net that will handle the largest fish you are likely to catch. Many rivers hold heavy trout in excess of 20 inches, so the frame of the net should be sturdy and the net bag at least 22 inches deep.

Figure 5.11   The tail-outs of big pools are ideal places to fish streamers at dawn and dusk.

Wading and Safety

The water fished by this method can be among the most dangerous of trout waters to the wading angler. The same depth and fast currents that have led to adjustments in basic fishing techniques also lead to adjustments in wading. Felt soles and a wading staff may no longer offer sufficient protection. You will need to add some type of metal-bottomed footwear to further reduce the likelihood of slipping. The type I prefer, Stream Cleats, has metal affixed to the bottom of rubber rainshoes which are pulled on over your fishing shoes or boots. A flotation vest offers an additional form of protection and may save your life should you lose footing in fast, heavy water.

In my estimation the most versatile concept in wading gear involves the use of sturdy, felt-soled wading shoes (e.g., James Scott) over latex stocking-foot waders, such as those made by Seal Dri. Latex has no seams that leak, and when ripped can be patched

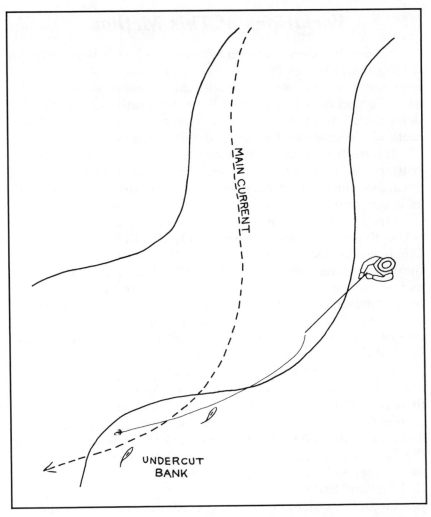

MAIN CURRENT

UNDERCUT
BANK

Figure 5.12 Undercut banks provide the opportunity to learn something about streamer fishing.

within a few moments on the stream. The stretchy nature of this material also affords more comfort than most other waders, particularly heavy boot-foot types. Of course their chest height enables you to wade deeper and reach more water than with hip waders. Seal Dris are more comfortable during warm weather than expensive neoprene waders, and when used over modern thick pile bibs, remain comfortable in cold conditions.

Variations of This Method

No one has done more to systematize heavy-water nymph fishing than Charles Brooks. One of the most enjoyable days I have spent on trout water was with this knowledgeable, friendly man. I regret only that I didn't have the forethought to film his demonstration of the "Brooks Method." Variations of this method are discussed in some detail in his books.

This method for fishing big nymphs also works with streamers—patterns tied to imitate small fish. In imitating the movements of small fish, the fly is typically activated rather than "dead drifted" as is commonly done when imitating nymphs.

One of the most innovative streamer fishermen in the West is Dan Byford, the creator of the highly effective Zonker pattern. Dan feels that a streamer should have three things—a convincing minnow outline, flash to reflect light, and motion in slow water as well as fast. He uses sinking lines because he wants a minnow imitation to spurt and stop, not rise and fall. If initially unsuccessful, Dan first varies the depth he is fishing and then the rate of retrieve. When he finally decides to try a different fly, he is likely to change the size rather than the color or pattern.

A specialized variation of this technique is to fish streamers under the banks of meandering streams. Your presentation of the fly may be little more than placing a loose pile of line directly up-current from the bank you intend to fish under. As the line sinks, it should drift well back under the bank. You fish by stripping the fly back upstream erratically through the hidden lie. Even in such protected holds, the fishing is usually best at dawn and dusk. Dick Holland first introduced me to this type of fishing in Oregon years ago. He took more and bigger fish than I did that evening, and as we walked back toward the car, I was feeling disgruntled that I hadn't done better. Then a strange thing happened—a mosquito flew into my ear and started burrowing toward my brain. It penetrated beyond the reach of my finger, and for the life of me, I couldn't recall the internal anatomy of the human ear. As we continued walking, all I could think of was the prospect of spending half the night finding a hospital to have that blasted mosquito removed. Then, just as our parked car came into view, the mosquito somehow managed to fly out of my ear. Though nothing had changed my fishing luck, my attitude improved dramatically. It's amazing how often we limit our pleasure by setting high expectations that can't always be met.

Selected Readings

Anderson, G. (1985, May). Early-season nymphing. *Fly Fisherman*.

Brooks, C.E. (1974). *The trout and the stream*. New York: Crown.

Brooks, C.E. (1976). *Nymph fishing for larger trout*. New York: Crown.

Wixom, H. (1975). How to fish swift water. *Cord Sport Facts— Fishing Report*.

Chapter **6**

Lake Fishing With Sinking Fly Lines: Going Down After Them

*L*ake-dwelling trout do not always feed at the surface. Frequently they may feed so deep that the fly fishing methods described in chapter 3 no longer work. Under such conditions, many "generalists" among the angling fraternity soon put their spin-fly rods to the use for which they seem designed—spin fishing. However, the person who is deeply committed to fly fishing, who loves the feel of a fly rod, simply changes from a floating fly line to a sinking fly line.

When trout are not rising in lakes, you face the problem of finding them. Surface rises let you *know* that the water you fish contains trout. But when fish are no longer visible, you begin to *hope* the water you cast to contains trout. This situation is typical of mountain lakes when the bright light of midday induces the trout to seek the protection of deep water. These trout may continue to feed, but now look for subsurface food.

Even when fish are feeding near the surface, a strong wind moves your floating fly line and fly unnaturally, with the result

Figure 6.1 When lake-dwelling trout don't rise, a sinking fly line may be necessary to catch them.

that trout begin to ignore the fly. A slow-sinking or intermediate fly line will cut down through the water enough to avoid being pushed around by the wind and yet permit you to fish a fly near the surface. This is only one of the conditions that requires you to have a sinking line when fly fishing in lakes.

I remember with chagrin my first exposure to little Martis Creek Lake near Truckee, California shortly after it opened to no-kill fly fishing. Frank Collin was anxious to have me fish an effective technique he had put together there, but somehow forgot to mention it involved the use of a sinking line. It turned out that Frank had a spare, but we still ended up one sinking line short in our party. As a charitable gesture I agreed to start out with a floating line. By the time someone offered to let me use a sinking line, the action was 90% over. If I had that day to live over, I doubt very much that I would have started with a floating line.

Rigging Adaptations

Our general-purpose fly rod performs adequately in this type of fly fishing. Many lake specialists are backpacking anglers who prefer that the cases for their fly rods not extend beyond the height of their backpacks. Therefore backpacking fly rods typically break down into three, four, or five pieces, and are much more enjoyable rods to cast than spin-fly combination rods.

The type of sinking line selected may depend on the characteristics of a particular lake you fish on a regular basis; some lakes slope more gradually near the shore than others, for example. If you fish a number of different lakes on the same trip, you gain flexibility by carrying at least slow-sinking and fast-sinking lines in addition to the basic floating line. If you want to start with one general-purpose sinking line for mountain lakes, I would suggest one with a moderate sink rate, such as a Scientific Angler, Wet Cel II. To conserve space, some backpackers use only 30-foot shooting-taper lines and carry the extra lines coiled up. Held in these coils by short pieces of pipe cleaner and having a pre-tied loop in the heavy end, these short lines can be changed quickly while fishing. You will probably find that a number 7 shooting-taper balances best with a number 6 fly rod, because there is almost no line weight to be cast beyond the first 30 feet of fly line. Full-length fly lines continue to have more weight beyond this point.

There is nothing sacred about 30 feet of line. In fact many accomplished double-haul casters prefer 35- to 45-foot lengths. These casters have the ability to control the extra line beyond the rod tip and are able to pick up additional casting distance with it. The added length in a 45-foot line also makes it possible to roll cast farther. On the other hand, some backpackers prefer ultra-short 25-foot shooting-tapers because of limited back casting room.

There is considerable variation in leader lengths used by sinking line anglers. Though I have recommended using short leaders with sinking lines in fast moving water, I recommend using long leaders when fishing such lines in still water. Here the thick line precedes the fly through the water being fished, so the line needs to be removed some distance from the fly. I see many successful

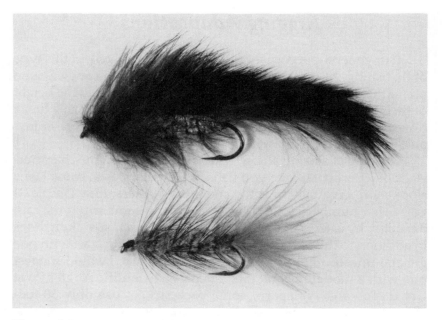

Figure 6.2   The Stripped-Hair Matuka (top) and Woolly-Bugger are effective sunken flies in still water. The latter's ability to pass for leech, minnow, and damsel nymph provides the general appeal needed when searching for fish.

lake specialists using leaders 12 feet long and longer with 5X or 6X tippets and small nymphs in the size 14 to 18 range.

When considering leaders to use with sinking lines, it's easy to overlook the importance of the leader butt. Without giving it much thought, people tend to stay with the basic advice given by tackle shop personnel and use a relatively thick leader butt (e.g., .021 to .025 of an inch) for its casting qualities. But when fishing with sinking lines, you want the leader to sink too and thick leader material is more buoyant than thin material. If your leader butt sinks more slowly than your fly line and fly, a "camel's hump" forms which detracts from your ability to sense a trout's grab. In this type of fishing my leader butt is usually about .017 of an inch in diameter; it certainly casts well enough and fishes much better than a thicker material.

With slow-sinking lines in particular, I feel it is important that your line and leader sink in a relatively straight configuration, because in shallow water trout often pick up your fly as it sinks. Thus your flies should have some weight so that they are presented

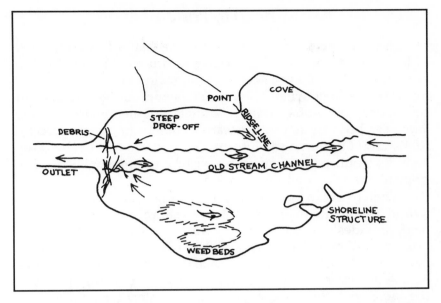

Figure 6.3   A sketch of lake features from a high overlook records the "big picture" that is not visible when fishing.

at a somewhat deeper level than the line is moving through the water.

However, with fast-sinking lines the best fishing usually occurs after the line has reached the bottom (or level to be fished). Here the fly typically has no weight so it floats slightly above the bottom, visible to nearby trout.

Some of the same "searching" patterns that we discussed in relation to stream fishing are effective in lakes. The subtle-toned Hare's Ear Nymph resembles a variety of the common, small-sized life forms found in lakes, including mayfly nymphs, caddis-fly larvae and pupae, scud, and water boatmen. Big impression-istic nymphs or Woolly-Worms sometimes cover a range of the larger trout food in lakes, including dragonfly nymphs, bait fish, and leeches. You can also find fly patterns that imitate each of these items specifically. These trout foods migrate through the water and usually are best imitated when pulled along behind sinking lines. Trout food that moves more vertically through the water, such as water boatmen, emerging mayfly nymphs, or midge pupae, are best imitated by a fly suspended from a float-ing line as discussed in chapter 11.

The Approach

The trail into a remote lake sometimes affords an overview of the water to be fished. You may find it worthwhile to stop at such places to draw a sketch of the main features of the lake for later reference when fishing. Inlets and outlets, points and coves, deep drop-offs, stream channels, submerged ridge lines, and weed beds are among the features that contribute to successful fishing. Of course any information you can obtain about the lake, its trout, or food chain by writing the managing agency prior to the trip is all to the good.

When trying to locate trout with a sinking line, you will want to find a spot with deep water close to shore; sometimes a steep bank provides this, but interferes with a back cast. A protruding point of land may also be a good place to start, and not primarily because back casts are easier to make there, but because you may be able to fish over two different groups of cruising fish from the same spot. Some experienced lake anglers have found that trout cruising a shoreline will turn around and go back the other way upon reaching the submerged point or ridge, rather than continue straight ahead into deeper water or make the sharp turn necessary to continue around the ridge. Trout cruising to the same ridge from the opposite direction are also likely to turn around and go back the way they came, thereby providing you with the second group of fish.

A strong wind may chase you to a protected cove, though there are several different theories about how to fly fish in the wind. When possible, I prefer to move to a shoreline that permits me to cast into the wind. Though casting range is reduced by doing this, any insects on the water will be blown toward you and will become concentrated close to your shore. Also, the wave action sometimes stirs up additional food from the shallow bottom there. Trout learn to find concentrations of food and, if not foraging actively, will face into the current from where their food and your artificial fly are coming. So the wind can be made to work for you.

Marv Taylor, one of the better known lake flyrodders in the Rocky Mountain area, follows similar thinking in working submerged shorelines during windy conditions. He believes that trout will move to the protected side of submerged ridges, face the current, and let the wind bring food to them.

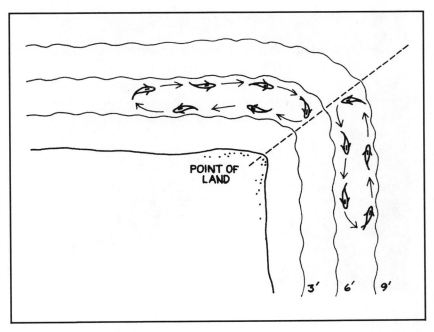

POINT OF
LAND

3'   6'   9'

Figure 6.4 A point of land may place you within reach of two groups of cruising fish.

Casting Techniques

One thing you can do when faced with the problem of locating trout in a lake is to sample various depths. Another approach, if you are limited to wading or bank fishing, is to cover as much distance as possible. This means casting a long line and fishing long drifts. The goal of extending your fishable range may lead you to learn the double haul, a technique that increases casting distance, some say by up to 30 percent over what can be obtained with the rod hand alone.

In the double haul, the line hand contributes to distance and line speed by pulling or hauling line twice during the cast—once as the rod hand applies power to the back cast and again as it applies power to the forward cast. After the second pull, the line hand releases its grip so that the line at the angler's feet is free to move up through the guides of the rod to follow that which is already moving toward the middle of the lake.

Figure 6.5 An increase in wind may cause fish to move to the protected side of submerged ridges.

Figure 6.6 Double-hauling adds distance to your casts. Here the downward pull of the line hand (first haul) has contributed to the bend in the rod during the back cast.

Figure 6.7   As the fly rod unloads, the line hand is drifting back up toward the rod hand.

Figure 6.8   As the line straightens in back, the angler is ready to begin moving both hands again: The rod hand will make the forward cast as the line hand pulls down a second time.

Figure 6.9 The forward cast and second haul have been completed and the line has been released. Note that the excess line, which has been on the water in front of the angler, is now rapidly disappearing out through the rod's guides.

When using a sinking line, you combine the double haul with a roll cast. The double haul provides the distance and the roll cast efficiently returns the sunken line to the surface for the next double haul. Thus, the whole sinking line doesn't have to be stripped in, but can be recast when 30 feet of line is still beyond the rod tip.

The double haul requires enough coordination between both arms that personal assistance should be sought when first learning the movements. If personal instruction is not available at a local tackle shop or fly fishing club, you might benefit from reading an article written by Mel Krieger or by seeing his excellent video, *The Essence of Fly Casting* (Sonoma Video Productions, Sebastopol, CA). Mel has developed a part method, or "pantomime" method, that simplifies the learning of this cast. This method and the movements involved are laid out systematically in the Winter 1980 issue of *Flyfisher*.

Figure 6.10   A submerged rod tip assures the precise movement of a fly fished on a sinking line.

Casting into the wind, as suggested earlier in this chapter, requires some modification in technique. The double haul is useful in this situation because it increases line speed, which contributes to your ability to cut through wind. With or without the ability to double haul, you can also fight the wind by using a casting variation referred to as the ''butt cast.'' In this variation your casting hand drives downward more than usual so as to get as much flex out of your rod's butt section as possible. This variation is most apparent when contrasted to that employed in casting a dry fly with a short line, when only the tip of the fly rod bends appreciably. To become versatile with a fly rod, you should practice casting off the tip of the rod as well as using the entire rod in butt casting. Both variations have important uses.

Line-Handling and Fishing Techniques

The basic technique for locating the depth at which trout are feeding is to count while the line is sinking. The count ends when

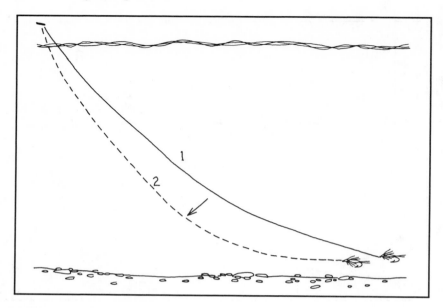

Figure 6.11   Sinking line sag: With rod tip fished above the water, stripping in line (1) reduces subsurface slack and moves the fly a little. Between strips (2), the line sag reforms and the fly moves a little more. Fishing with the tip submerged decreases the sag and increases your control over the movements of the fly.

you begin the retrieve. Different depths are sampled systematically by varying this count till you begin to get strikes. Sometimes it makes sense to start shallow and add to the count as you fish progressively deeper. Usually, however, you count the fly down to the bottom initially and back the count off a few numbers to fish just off the bottom.

Immediately after the cast, you should lower the tip of the rod. When sinking lines are used, you should consider submerging the rod up to half its length. I always thought this technique was unnecessary until fellow fly fishing teacher, Scott Henderson, and I conducted some experiments in a swimming pool. Only then did I realize the extent to which the submerged rod tip adds to your control over the exact movements of the fly. Like many anglers, I had assumed that stripping in 8 inches of line with the line hand would move the fly 8 inches at the same rate of movement. To my surprise, this happened only with the tip submerged. Even with the tip held a couple of inches above the surface and 40 feet of fly line out, an 8-inch strip of line resulted in moving the fly an average of only 4 inches. What happens is that slack forms in the submerged line, and the first 4 inches of the pull accomplish little more than tightening the line. Only the second 4 inches of the strip actually move the fly 4 inches. Then, between strips, the fly may drift a few more inches as the line accumulates slack once again.

It's even worse when the tip is held 2 feet above the surface. A series of 8-inch strips, with momentary pauses interspersed between, is transmitted as almost constant, steady movement of the fly rather than the expected stop-and-go jerks. You might just as well use a slow hand-twist retrieve. If you are interested in imitating the specific movements of small, invertebrate life, it would be worth your time to observe your fly moving through the depths of a swimming pool.

Some fly patterns seem to be most effective with particular retrieves. For example, a Matuka type of streamer looks very enticing when moved erratically in still water—it looks good even between jerks when completely still in the water. On the other hand, a streamer with marabou tied in only at the head of the fly looks ridiculous sitting dead in quiet water, with the marabou separated from the fly's body. It looks much more appealing (to the human eye at least) when permitted to move continuously. The currents of streams undoubtedly contribute to the effectiveness of this type of fly.

If forced to limit myself to one fly for this type of fly fishing, it would be a dark Woolly-Bugger because of its enticing movements through the water. After sinking it to the bottom, I like to give it a couple of quick jerks to get the attention of any trout in the neighborhood. Then I start crawling this fly along the bottom very slowly by means of short, frequent strips of line. If this doesn't provide action, I will alternate this retrieve with one that features long, erratic spurts of the fly. If I can't hook the fish that begin to hit it, I continue the drift, nonetheless. Jack Shaw, the lake specialist from British Columbia, has alerted us to the fact that soft-hitting trout will often return to our fly and take it more violently from a different angle.

Figure 6.12   Trudging through the weed beds should be done carefully as they may conceal drop-offs.

Hooking and Landing the Fish

Fishing with a submerged rod tip minimizes the amount of slack in the line and thus contributes to quickness in setting the hook. Some lake anglers avoid striking upward with the rod because they feel most of the power is absorbed in lifting an inert line from the surface. They believe that rod power is transmitted more efficiently to the fly by moving the line laterally against water drag. So they set the hook with a short rod movement to one side.

When using a sinking line in lakes, you may find yourself hooking larger fish than you are accustomed to. Sometimes large fish in lakes move slowly when hooked and panic only when first led into shallow water. Under these conditions it is wise to expect not to beach the fish the first time it is worked into shallow water. Expect it to bolt into deep water with renewed energy, and you won't make the mistake of trying to overpower it at this critical moment—when a tippet can easily be broken.

Wading and Safety

When wading in lakes you should always be alert for sudden drop-offs, or unevenness in soft-bottomed areas. These drop-offs may be concealed under weed beds you are walking on or by water that has been discolored by your movements. You should move carefully when wading in unfamiliar surroundings.

Variations of This Method

You can build on this sinking line method by experimenting with different lines and retrieves until you find the best combination for your particular lake. Even this may vary as the season progresses. If you take to this form of fishing, you will feel the need to cover more water and will obtain a float tube, small boat, or both. As an added bonus, you will find that many good trout lakes are usually closer to metropolitan areas than are good trout streams.

Selected Readings

Baker, C. (1981, November/December). Down, down, down. *Flyfishing the west*.

Bates, J. (1979). *Streamers & Bucktails—The big fish flies*. New York: Knopf.

Blanton, D. (1979, Early Season). Sinking lines. *Fly Fisherman*.

Blanton, D. (1979, Mid–Season). Sinking lines for stillwater trout. *Fly Fisherman*.

Havstad, J. (1979, Fall). Sink rate of sinking lines. *The Flyfisher*.

Janssen, H. (1980, Late Spring). The life of a damsel. *Angler*.

Janssen, H. (1984, March). The leech. *Fly Fisherman*.

Krieger, M. (1980, Winter). DownUp and the double haul. *Flyfisher*.

Moyle, P., & Baltz, D. (1980). Stillwaters west. In J. Merwin (Ed.), *Stillwater trout*. Garden City, NY: Doubleday.

Chapter 7

Short-Line, Wet Fly Fishing: A Transition to Upstream Nymphing

*F*or many people the most enjoyable way to fish "pocket water" is with a dry fly, as described in chapter 4. However, I believe that the most productive way to fish this water is with a sunken fly—either a wet fly or nymph. There are too many times throughout the day and too many days throughout the season that fish are reluctant to rise but can be taken with a fly fished near the bottom. And it took me many years to prove to myself that the better fish in this type of cascading water, the ones I most want to hook, are primarily bottom feeders—especially in the deeper, protected holds.

For years I fished dry flies only and gave little thought to wet fly anglers, until I saw some highly skilled short-line nymphers at work. I soon realized that the added dimension of depth brought with it some intriguing challenges as well as the increased action. The challenge of presenting the fly with the optimal combination of depth, naturalness, and line control is more involved than you would think based on the short lengths of line typically used.

The short length and narrowness of the small pools as well as the extreme current variations in these restricted areas present some problems. How do you get the fly deep quickly and yet keep it moving naturally in the water? How do you detect strikes in pocket water without the advantage of seeing them on the surface? These problems require some adjustments in fishing technique as well as in tackle.

Rigging Adaptations

Some of the modifications in tackle that are suggested here are the same as those suggested for fishing pocket water with a dry fly. In both methods short casts are made to keep line from falling on the fast currents surrounding the small pools. It is this use of a short line that leads to modifications in fly rod and leader: The fly rod should be soft enough in action to "load" or flex in response to the weight of only a few feet of line. The leader must be kept short to provide as much line weight beyond the rod tip as possible to help power the short casts. Typically, such leaders range from 6 to 7-1/2 feet long.

Although a fly is fished deep with this method, floating fly lines are the rule. Depth is achieved by applying weight to the leader and the fly, rather than with a sinking line, which is more appropriate in broad expanses of water or when the current is less swift.

I recommend to my beginning students that they buy a package or two of flat lead wire strips (i.e., twistons) and that they spiral-wrap four or five turns of this lead wire and crimp the ends 18 inches above the fly. Wine bottle lead seals could also be cut into strips for this purpose. The flies I use with this method also have a half-dozen turns of 2-amp lead fuse wire under the body. So a moderate amount of weight is distributed in two places. If this weight were concentrated in one place, casting would become unwieldy, and the drift would become less natural.

For anglers already experienced in other fly fishing methods, I suggest replacing the weight on the leader with a second weighted fly. With two flies you can experiment continually with two different patterns and two different depths.

Beginners may use the two-fly rigging, but usually they either dislike losing two good flies at once or shy away from a rigging

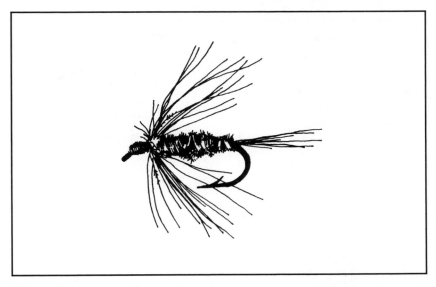

Figure 7.1   Sparsely dressed, well-chewed Gray-Hackle Peacock resembles both aquatic and terrestrial insects.

that increases their likelihood of getting tangled or wrapped around everything within casting distance.

A simple way of rigging two flies is to use a blood knot to connect the last two sections of leader tippet material—a 1X (.010 inch) to a 3X (.008 inch) tippet section, for example. In tying this blood knot, the 1X material is tied so as to leave 6 to 8 inches of material extending beyond the knot. When tightened, this piece is not trimmed off and becomes the dropper strand. If tied correctly, it should extend straight out from the leader. Its stiffness keeps it far enough away from the leader to prevent some tangling.

At the end of the dropper strand, I often tie on a light-colored fly to imitate the lighter color tones that are characteristic of a variety of emerging insects. This is logical since the dropper is closer to the surface than is the "point fly." A Leisenring Spider, tied with a body of rabbit fur and hackled with grouse or partridge, is one of my favorites. Often I contrast this with a dark pattern on the tail or point fly fished near the bottom. My favorite fly for this purpose is a weighted Gray-Hackle Peacock—as good a pocket water fly as there is, in my estimation. The peacock herl

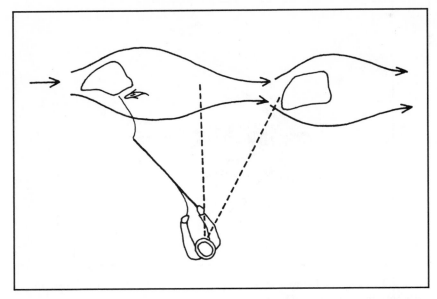

Figure 7.2 "Bisecting the fishable drift" means positioning yourself with half the fishable water upstream of you and half downstream.

makes a buggy-looking body that reflects light and appears translucent in sunlight. It also resembles a variety of common terrestrial and aquatic insects, including some cased-caddis larvae. In rugged Western streams, a stiffer hackle is used for these flies than in the soft-hackled patterns preferred by many Eastern anglers.

The Approach

Most experienced pocket-water anglers, whether they use surface or sunken flies, take advantage of the concealment afforded by approaching an upstream-facing trout from behind and casting up and across stream.

While I do this in my own fishing, I have found that fishing upstream angles with a sunken fly is too difficult for many beginners. There is just too much to learn at once about line-handling and strike detection. So I have developed a simplified approach

Figure 7.3   An across-stream "transition" to upstream nymphing affords the opportunity for both upstream and downstream fishing angles.

to help make a smooth transition from downstream wet fly fishing to upstream wet fly fishing.

This "transition" method retains some of the familiar techniques of the basic down-and-across swing, while introducing some of the elements of upstream nymphing. This is accomplished by fishing across-stream angles, rather than upstream angles. In so doing, you eliminate line-handling operations such as stripping line in or feeding it out; you can fish the entire drift with the same amount of line.

What I do is find a pocket that can be approached from across stream and wade with the student to a point directly across stream from the pocket, so that exactly half of its fishable drift is upstream of the student, and half is downstream. I refer to this positioning concept as "bisecting the fishable drift."

The student casts up and across to the head of the pool and learns upstream techniques during the first half of the drift, and still has the familiar downstream fishing angles for the last half. There is a good chance that fish will continue to be hooked on the

Figure 7.4 Experienced pocket-water anglers typically fish such water by moving and casting in an upstream direction.

downstream side of the drift while students are putting together the more complicated upstream concepts. Eventually they begin to hook fish on the upstream side of the drift and gain the confidence needed to attempt drifts that are entirely upstream of them.

Students frequently ask me how close they should stand to the fishable water in a small pool. It's easy enough to answer, ''as close as possible without spooking trout,'' but a learner has to spend time on the stream to fully understand what is involved. If you don't have a fishing friend to assist you in this, it may be worth your while to hire a fishing guide for a day. A competent guide can give you enough assistance and instruction in one day to help you overcome a number of shortcomings in your technique.

If no guide is available, you should keep a few things in mind about positioning yourself. First, there may be one best place to stand to cast to a particular piece of water. If your fly lands short of the mark in the fast water on your side of the pocket, you may need to take a step or two toward the fishable water. On the other hand, if you see fish dart around in the pocket, you have probably spooked them by being too close.

Figure 7.5 Stopping the rod high on the tuck cast creates the high pivot point that allows the weighted fly to swing back toward you under the line.

Each pocket is unique to a degree. Those with large areas of quiet water give the trout the best chance to see you. Any turbulent water on your side of the pocket can help conceal you from the trout. When in doubt, keep low.

A single step to one side or the other can be important in decreasing the amount of glare you see on the water. A second step can make it much easier to see your leader and detect strikes.

Exact positioning before the cast can add to the number of fish you catch or at least to the number of strikes you are able to detect.

Casting Techniques

Some flyrodders dislike fishing short-line methods, especially when some weight is added to the terminal tackle. Yet if you enjoy wading mountain streams and catching large trout on a fly in mixed currents, the chances are you will add this method to your arsenal.

Figure 7.6 Overpowering the cast helps to "tuck" the fly back toward you so it sinks quickly.

Many people practice casting on a lawn, usually with from 25 to 50 feet of fly line beyond the rod tip. Yet it is quite a different matter to prepare students for a pocket water experience. Pretrip casting practice should include some time with weight on the leader and fly and only 10 to 20 feet of line beyond the rod tip. With an emphasis on accuracy—a waste basket makes a convenient target—you begin to realize what is necessary to cast well in cascading water.

This emphasis on accuracy has to do with the extreme current variation that sometimes characterizes pocket water. A fly that lands 6 inches off target may drift much faster than you like, and the speed your fly moves through the water is directly related to the number of trout that move to your fly. It's amazing how trout will sometimes ignore one presentation after another until

Figure 7.7 A low follow-through on the cast provides line control rather than depth. The whole leader lands and starts to sink at the same time—with little slack.

your fly finally lands in the narrow slot of slow water you have been aiming for; only then comes the hit. This is related to the fact that "naturalness" of drift in deep nymphing is a matter of matching the speed of bottom currents, which are typically much slower than those at the water's surface. Naturalness under these conditions may be achieved by adding, rather than removing, terminal weight. As pointed out here, it is also achieved by accurate casting.

A "specialty cast" that is useful in pocket water, when it is important to get the fly deep quickly, is commonly known as the tuck cast. The idea of this cast is to get the fly into the water first in such a way that the leader doesn't restrict the penetration of the fly down through the water. There are two important elements to the tuck cast. First, you overpower the forward cast so that the leader not only straightens, but continues beyond straightening, until the fly has swung under the line and "tucked" back toward you. Second, the forward cast is stopped early so that the rod tip is high (i.e., 10 to 11 o'clock). A high rod tip enables the tuck to be completed above the surface of the water.

Figure 7.8   Raising the rod after the cast helps control above-surface slack as the fly approaches you.

Line-Handling and Fishing Techniques

Sometimes it's more important to cast for "line control" than for depth. In fishing an upstream-cast sunken fly back toward you, you want to minimize the slack in the line and leader, both above and below the water's surface, because you must see rather than feel the indication of a strike. This is discussed in more detail in the next section. The implication is that the cast must be powered hard enough to straighten the leader on and into the water, so it is relatively straight when the sinking fly is grabbed by a trout.

The weight on the terminal tackle, which provides depth to the drifting fly, also contributes to line control because its downward pull on the leader removes slack.

I see many beginners lose line control immediately by casting more line than is necessary to fish a particular spot. If extra line is cast, it forms hidden slack in the leader below the surface, which removes your ability to detect strikes. The two-fly concept discussed earlier reduces this possibility as long as you keep the top or dropper fly visible, near the surface. It is also a convenient check on the amount of leader that lies below. Thus when fishing your leader almost vertically into pocket water that averages about 2 feet in depth, your point (bottom) fly is ideally located about 18 inches below the dropper fly being fished near the surface.

Though less common, it is also possible to err by casting too little line for the water being fished. You can check your tendency to do this by watching to make sure the fly doesn't jerk upward through the water as you lift the rod tip after the cast.

Once the cast has been made, the line can be controlled by the actions of your line hand, rod hand, or both acting together. As in other upstream fly fishing methods, the line hand does its job by gathering line off the water in pace with the oncoming current.

However, it is the work of the rod hand that is distinctive in this method. Immediately after the cast, the rod tip is smoothly lifted, which tends to straighten the line falling to the water's surface. The shorter the line being fished, the higher the rod tip is held and the more vertical the line and leader drop to and through the surface. In very close fishing, the leader cuts directly through the surface without any of it lying on the water. Sometimes the rod tip is raised during the drift, as the fly approaches you, and then lowered again if you decide to continue fishing the fly downstream away from you. If you fail to raise the tip immediately after the cast when fishing this technique, you will lose many fish without even being aware that your fly has been taken.

Frequently beginners find it difficult to learn both the line-gathering and the rod-raising operations at the same time. For this reason, I often start students fishing this technique with only the rod hand—learning first to control slack by raising and lowering the rod tip. When confident with this, they are ready to learn to use the line hand and eventually to combine the two.

As the rod tip is raised, it must be steadied as soon as possible. Then any unusual movement in your leader has been caused from below—by a trout or rock that has momentarily interrupted the movement of your fly. Whichever it is, you should set the hook immediately.

Though held steady, the rod tip is moved gradually to remain pointed toward your fly throughout the drift. This provides an element of naturalness to the drift as the fly is free to move directly

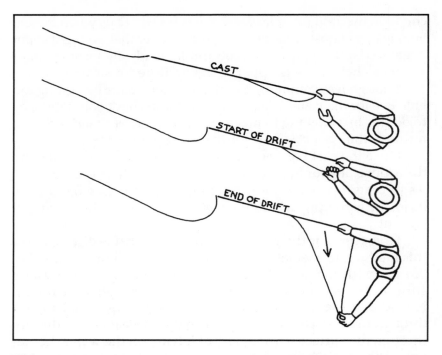

Figure 7.9   The late Ted Fay's line-handling technique increases hooking percentages in pocket water. The line hand release on the cast enabled him to pick line up again next to the rod, affording the longest possible distance for a single draw of the line. The fly can be activated during the drift by "feathering the line" as it is drawn to the side.

downstream as if unattached to any leader. This "dead drift" dimension disappears quickly if the rod tip is allowed to precede the fly downstream or lag behind it.

A rod tip that lags behind the fly results in a tight line, which in turn brings the fly up to the surface when you want it drifting deep. A rod tip that leads the fly downstream may soon be pulling it faster than the speed of the current and therefore faster than the trout's food usually moves.

There are times, however, when it pays to pull the fly slightly faster than the current (or slightly across the current)—sacrificing some naturalness for increased line control. When fish are taking softly, for example, or when glare makes it difficult to see your leader, the increased line tension from pulling the fly provides the earliest possible feel of a take. There are days when this tight

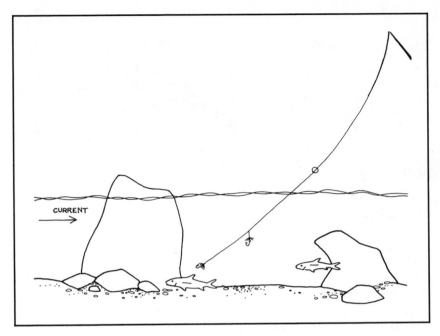

CURRENT

Figure 7.10 When visibility is limited, a small piece of bright yarn attached to the leader may help you detect when a trout has picked up your fly.

line modification will result in fewer strikes, but a higher hooking percentage and more fish to catch and release.

This tight line adaptation is also useful when current variation is not extreme. By pulling slightly on the fly throughout the drift so it moves gradually across stream toward you, the leader is kept fairly straight despite some current variation. This is an entirely different approach from keeping your leader and fly out of the fast water. In the first case you are fishing through current variation; in the second, you are reaching over, and thus avoiding, the current variation.

Hooking and Landing the Fish

The transition from downstream sunken fly fishing to upstream sunken fly fishing is a transition from tactile strike detection to visual strike detection. A fly line that has tightened downstream of you permits strikes to be felt quickly, whereas a line moving

Figure 7.11   When nymphing upstream with a short line, watch your leader close to the water for the earliest indication of strikes.

toward you from upstream tends to form slack, which gives the trout time to spit out the fly before the feel reaches your hands. Here you sense the strike sooner by seeing an unusual movement in the leader, before it even reaches the fly line.

Though excessive slack is to be avoided, there should be a slight bow in the line and leader dropping from the high rod tip. This bow or sag in the leader disappears whenever the movement of the fly is interrupted—whether by trout, snag, or sudden change in current speed. I like to watch my leader as close to the water as possible for the first indication of this straightening or tightening. If glare or shade makes it difficult to see your leader, tie a small piece of red yarn onto it to be visible about 6 inches above the water's surface when fishing this method.

In upstream sunken fly fishing, I set the hook by separating my hands—moving the rod up and to one side while pulling the line down and away to the other. Pulling with the line hand alone won't set the hook if enough slack has formed in the line. And setting with the rod hand alone makes it too easy to overreact

Figure 7.12 Oversized pants on top of lightweight stocking-foot waders protect the waders from tearing.

and break fine tippets when big fish hit on a short line. I do set the hook with the rod hand alone when my whole rod arm is extended to reach a distant pocket or when using only my rod hand to fish.

A big fish hooked in cascading water can be expected to move downstream through the entire series of rapids. In this situation you try to wade ashore and scramble down the bank with rod held high to keep as much line off the water as possible. When the line catches on a rock, it becomes a race to free the line before the fish can free itself. You look downstream for a pool large enough to catch up with the fish and beach or net it.

Wading and Safety

The most common wading problem I have when moving up-stream through cascading water is tripping on submerged rocks. Falling upstream in shallow water is not usually dangerous, but

Figure 7.13   Short-line tactics may be applied to the slower seams in heavy, turbulent runs. Note how an extended arm and long rod contribute to reaching beyond fast water.

can lead to scraped shins. This happens to me through over-confidence and by ''striding''—alternating one foot in front of the other. It's safer to shuffle crablike, keeping the same foot upstream when the water is fast and deep.

Wading staffs and felt-soled footgear are standard equipment for pocket-water anglers. The wading staff is particularly useful in locating odd-shaped or protruding rocks beneath frothy or discolored water and in dislodging flies snagged on obstructions.

Variations of This Method

One particularly effective form of this method involving the use of two flies and short leaders has been popularized over the years by Ted Fay on the Upper Sacramento and McCloud Rivers in California. Fishing the two-fly rig enabled Ted to experiment continually with fly patterns and learn which flies work best there throughout the season. For decades Ted Fay gave of his knowledge willingly. His assistance and friendliness endeared Ted to thousands of fly fishers who happened to pass through the town of Dunsmuir. Ted found that his unique fly patterns and techniques worked as well in the East as they do in freestone streams of the West.

When you become efficient in controlling line and detecting strikes in this short-line method, you are ready to attempt the same with longer casts and techniques as described in chapter 10. The additional lengths of line coupled with increased terminal weight make long-line, upstream nymphing one of the most difficult fly fishing methods to master.

Selected Readings

Green, L. (1973, February). Nymphs plain and simple. *Field & Stream*.

Green, L. (1975, November/December). Ted Fay's deadly wet fly concept. *Angler*.

Humphreys, J. (1981). *Joe Humphreys' trout tactics*. Harrisburg, PA: Stackpole.

La Fontaine, G. (1980). The misunderstood caddis pupa. In Scientific Angler (Ed.), *Fly fishing handbook*. Point Pleasant, NJ: Aqua–Field.

Scott, J. (1979, November/December). The leisenring lift. *Fly-fishing the west*.

Up and Across Stream Dry Fly Fishing: Beyond Pocket Water

*T*he fishing techniques described in this chapter constitute what may be considered the "classic" method of fly fishing. To many old timers, this was the only method of fly fishing.

Though the fundamentals of upstream, dry fly fishing are frequently learned in pocket water with the short-line techniques described in chapter 4, most flyrodders associate dry fly fishing with longer pools and runs. Thus one envisions casts of 25 feet or more falling on moderately flowing riffles, quiet glides, or the long, narrow pools of small streams. The common ingredients of these water types are the presence of (a) relatively even water flow in which to lay out line, leader, and fly, and (b) relatively shallow water (e.g., between 1 and 4 feet) through which trout can easily rise to surface food.

Perhaps the most difficult problem you experience in learning this method is that of handling long lengths of upstream-cast line for the first time. This particular line control problem becomes most evident in the faster runs. However, the pleasure of laying

Figure 8.1   Shallow, relatively even-flowing water provides the opportunity to reach out with a dry fly.

out line in a delicate cast, the fascination of watching a dry fly bobbing toward you in the currents, and the thrill of a surface strike explain why so many people enjoy this form of fishing.

Rigging Adaptations

In this method there is no need to depart from the general-purpose fly rod, reel, and floating line suggested in chapter 1. Nine-foot leaders are popular in long pools, often tapered down to 4X or 5X and used with size 14 dry flies. Toward the end of the day, however, you may choose to switch to a larger fly as light fades. Reduced light intensity, and the increased insect activity associated with it, often make the trout less cautious.

The fly I am most likely to select for this method when there is no apparent hatch to match is a size 14 Elk Hair Caddis as designed by Al Troth of Dillon, Montana. It is a good general-purpose attractor that floats well and provides a convincing silhouette of downwing insects, including some terrestrials, stone-flies, and of course caddisflies. I always try to keep a stock of

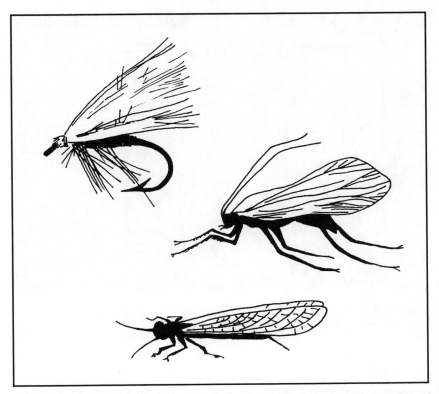

Figure 8.2   Swept-back hair wings of the Elk Hair Caddis give the downwing profile of adult caddisflies (top) and stoneflies (bottom).

this pattern in various sizes from 12 to 18 and tied with both dark and light elk hair.

In particularly quiet pools, 12-foot leaders provide a little extra distance between your fly and the relatively thick, visible fly line. Such water is more transparent so small tippets (e.g., 5X or 6X) and flies (e.g., size 16) will help fool trout that have extra time to scrutinize your offerings.

The Approach

If you park close to the stream, it may be worth your while to collect insects from streamside foliage before fishing. Large

Figure 8.3   Retrieving line into coils saves time when you need to wade 15 or 20 steps upstream between casts.

sweep nets that are associated with collecting butterflies some-times reveal the presence of heavy concentrations of terrestrials, such as carpenter ants, or of aquatic insects that have emerged recently. If you are unable to recognize the most common aquatic insects, at least you can select fly patterns that resemble those that are abundant on the foliage. An important part of this resemblance is the shape of the insect's wings. This wing shape also guides your learning of the most common insects. For example, the wings of an adult stonefly are folded back flat on its body. The wings of an adult caddisfly are also folded back—but in a roof or tent shape. Both are referred to as downwing flies in contrast to the mayfly duns, whose wings are upright at rest—like the sails of a sailboat. You can learn about these insects more quickly if you collect them in a small, watertight bottle or film container and take them to your local fly shop proprietor for identification.

In both pocket-water methods, I have suggested an upstream-wading, upstream-casting approach. This approach also works on the longer pools envisioned here, though you will want to

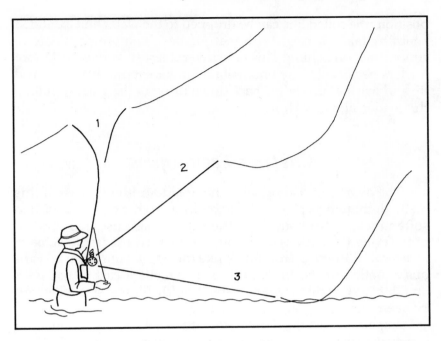

Figure 8.4   A fly's soft, fluttery drop to the water is achieved with a lowered back cast and raised forward cast.

stay farther back from the fish to conceal yourself and thus make longer casts.

You should look for casting positions that afford relatively even flow upstream on which to drift the line, leader, and fly. In such unbroken water you frequently have some choice of upstream casting angles, though a cast dropped directly upstream may "line the trout"—that is, place the fly line close enough over the fish to spook it.

A careless habit that you can pick up when fishing this method is to cast continuously while wading upstream. One consequence is to miss fish that strike when you are stumbling or concentrating on wading. Another is to trip and fall while watching the fly.

When you have to wade more than a few steps and are rigged with a leader not longer than 9 feet, you can stop fishing by retrieving line in large coils with the fly left hanging above the level of the water to stay dry. After wading to the next casting position, the coiled line can be dropped to the water and extended again by false casting. With feet planted, you are then able to concentrate on fishing. This time saver doesn't work with 12-foot leaders because the fly line will no longer extend out to the rod tip and will end up sliding back down through the guides, pulling the leader along with it.

Casting Techniques

The overhead cast remains the bread-and-butter cast of this method, though its plane is tilted backward whenever you wish to soften the drop of your fly to the water. I also use this concept of lowering the back cast and raising the forward cast to achieve a vertical, fluttering drop much like the egg-laying flight of various aquatic insects. In fact this is an excellent cast to use with an Elk Hair Caddis whenever small caddisflies or stoneflies can be seen egg-laying at the surface.

A specialty cast that I use frequently when fishing this method is a curve cast. Throwing an upstream curve in a cast that has been delivered up and across stream reduces the possibility of having the leader drift over the fish ahead of the fly (which can spook fish in quiet water). This curve cast also helps delay the onset of drag in tricky currents. To be effective, the curve should appear throughout the entire leader, something that becomes difficult to accomplish in leaders longer than about 9 feet.

The curve cast, however it is taught, is based on the principle that the line goes where the rod tip sends it. Beginners who understand this principle seem to learn the cast more quickly. I have them start the hand and rod moving toward their target at the beginning of the forward cast and, as quickly as possible, move the tip to one side or another. Typically, the farthest part of the line and the leader land pointing to the target, and a sharp angle in the line near the rod indicates where the tip was moved to the side. With practice, the rod tip movements are made more quickly and smoothly to form a gentle curve in the leader and line closer to the fly.

Eventually you may want to learn curve casts with the rod tip canted down to either side to slide the fly under overhanging foliage. This variation involves some overpowering so that the sideways loop not only straightens but reverses its curve before

Figure 8.5   Drop the fly rod down toward the horizontal plane to cast under overhanging foliage.

Figure 8.6   Then overpower the forward cast to bend the line and present the fly back under the branches.

Figure 8.7   Overpowering the off-side cast enables you to achieve a negative curve (i.e., curve to the left for a left-handed caster).

Figure 8.8   Foliage on your casting side can be countered by canting the rod so its tip and the fly line move back and forth on the stream side of your body. This useful technique is sometimes called an off-side cast.

Figure 8.9 Faint current tongues upstream to the right reveal several drift lanes that are slow enough to be fished from the same spot before wading farther upstream.

being dropped to the surface. If you are a right-handed caster facing upstream, you can use this ''positive'' curve cast to reach fish lying close to the bank off to your left. To accomplish this cast when the fish and bank are off to your right, you can tilt the rod over your head so that the tip is over your left shoulder. This ''off-side'' cast is also overpowered to produce an upstream curve.

Line-Handling and Fishing Techniques

''Fishing the rise'' is one of the traditional elements of up-stream dry fly fishing. In some privately controlled English streams, for example, you are allowed to cast only to rising fish. In such fishing you learn to present the fly slightly off to your side of the trout to keep the line and leader from drifting over it.

Fishing the rise is not always possible. You may know streams, such as the Upper Sacramento River, where there are days when trout are seldom seen rising yet will take a dry fly readily. Waiting for a fish to rise would only waste valuable fishing time. In a stream such as this, you get more action by "fishing the water"— fishing progressively upstream through promising looking runs.

With years of experience, you begin to know where in the pool the fish is most likely to rise and to which cast. I demonstrated this one day to Bob Dering, one of the capable fly fishermen who helps me teach classes on the Upper Sacramento. On this particular day, I wanted to get a photograph of a trout taking a dry fly, and soon came within view of a riffle that "couldn't miss." Bob was skeptical but took the camera, listened to my instructions for taking the picture, and crawled into position close to where I told him the fish would rise. After snapping the shutter, Bob's outcry was of such an irritated nature that I thought he had missed the shot. I was wrong. "Not only did you predict that a trout would rise, where it would rise, to which cast, and that you would hook it, but you predicted that I would get the picture," he exclaimed. Mostly Bob was annoyed that I had predicted his behavior. Undoubtedly I was a little lucky, though experience minimizes much of the guesswork. I had never fished that run before.

Though the upper reaches of a particular riffle may look to be the most promising water, the experienced upstream dry fly fisher learns to cover the downstream portions first, especially in clear, shallow pools where fish are easily spooked. When you cast to the downstream water first, fish startled by the landing of the fly or leader are likely to move to nearby cover without alarming the better fish farther upstream. However, when you attempt to bypass the tail of the pool, these same fish are apt to be startled by your silhouette or the fly line and are likely to bolt upstream in panic, thus "putting down" any fish feeding there.

When fishing up through a riffle, you typically move in stages, taking a few steps, then making a few casts. Your casts from a single location may sample several drift lanes and distances (through extending line). On each cast the fly is gently lifted off the water far enough upstream to keep any fish that have followed the fly from seeing you.

In slow-moving runs I sometimes gather in line by means of an old technique called the hand-twist retrieve which you may read about elsewhere. I don't emphasize its use in my teaching, because stripping in line from behind the rod hand is easier for beginners to learn and controls line better in fast currents, which makes it a more versatile technique.

Figure 8.10   This angler is beginning to fall behind in retrieving an upstream-cast line. Any slack that is allowed to build up beneath the rod tip detracts from the precise movements needed to set the hook effectively.

Hooking and Landing the Fish

Forty feet of line or more drifting on the water upstream of you usually forms some slack despite your best line-handling efforts. This being the case, your movements in setting the hook must be extensive enough to straighten the line as well as to move the fly. The more slack line that is on the water, the more extensive these movements must be. Thus it helps to fish this method with the rod tip low to the water so that you leave yourself as much upward distance as possible to raise your rod in setting the hook. However, if you get caught fishing with your rod tip up when the fish grabs, you may be forced to pull back with the rod to remove the slack. Unfortunately, this movement tends to break delicate tippets, especially on heavy fish. As mentioned before, the line hand helps tighten line by pulling downward as you set.

When I have hooked a good fish well upstream of me, I try to keep rod pressure on it in the hope that it will move away from this resistance—farther upstream. If this happens, the trout is moving against the force of the current as well as against the resistance in the fly rod and will soon tire itself. It should be brought to net quickly so it doesn't become overly exhausted.

If your trout jumps, and you have the presence of mind to think of it, you should lower the rod. This has the effect of giving a little line at a time when the trout's movement into the air may have added to the strain on the leader. Giving this line may also prevent the tippet from breaking if the fish should land on it.

Wading and Safety

In a previous chapter I mentioned the preferred "crablike" shuffling movements you should use when wading upstream. With a wading staff, you have the addition of a third "foot." In using these three wading feet, it is important to remember that two of them should always provide firm support while the other moves. I have slipped with a wading staff and realized it was almost always because I had been moving the staff and one of my feet at the same time. Also keep in mind that whenever you depend on the support of a staff held on your downstream side, you risk a disorienting head-downstream fall.

My staff is an old bamboo ski pole with the ring removed from the bottom. Occasionally I have used a dead limb for this purpose when making an unexpected crossing, but only after testing its strength by leaning hard against it.

Variations of This Method

The ability to fish this method effectively simplifies the learning of long-line, upstream nymphing as described in chapter 10. Much of the approach, the casting angles, the wading, and the line-handling are the same.

Selected Readings

Arbona, F. (1985, December). Feeding lanes. *Fly Fisherman*.

Fox, C. (1977). Upstream, the classic presentation. In J. Migel (Ed.), *The masters on the dry fly*. Philadelphia: Lippincott.

Goddard, J., & Clark, B. (1980). *The trout and the fly*. Garden City, NY: Doubleday.

Marinaro, V. (1970). *A modern dry-fly code*. New York: Crown.

Schwiebert, E. (1974, February). How I fish dry flies. *Sports Afield*.

Sosin, M. (1982, February). Brown trout breakthrough. *Sports Afield*.

Wilson, D. (1970). *Fishing the dry fly*. London: A. & C. Black.

Downstream Dry Fly Fishing: A Presentation for Educated Meadow-Stream Trout

*F*ishing a dry fish with a downstream-angled cast represents a departure from the dry fly theory and methods discussed thus far. This downstream dry fly method has become increasingly popular on some waters, most often on meadow streams inhabited by "educated" trout.

One of the problems that meadow-stream anglers face is how to catch trout that refuse to move out of extremely narrow feeding lanes of only a few inches. Often your fly must be dropped almost directly upstream of such trout. As an upstream caster you can no longer present the fly off to one side but must move your cast in closer to the fish because of the accuracy required. This increases the likelihood that part of your leader will drift over the trout before the fly arrives. Unfortunately, such trout often become leader shy and learn to refuse this presentation. So there

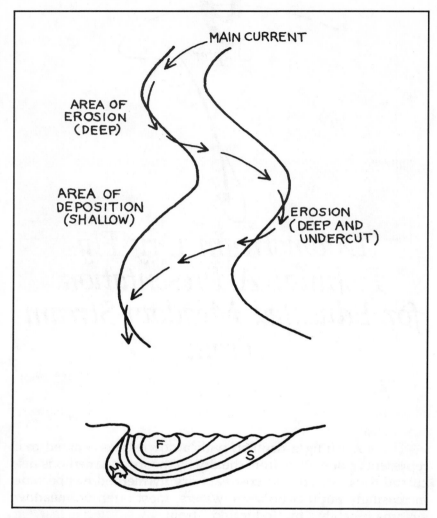

Figure 9.1   Deep trout holds may be formed wherever the main current of a meandering stream swings to the bank. The cross section of a typical under-cut bank shows the location of the fastest (F) and slowest (S) currents.

are times in which it pays to drift your fly down to the fish ahead of the leader—by quartering your cast down and across stream.

This downstream presentation may also be necessary to float a fly into a trout that has grown old by learning to feed in the midst of uneven currents. The fastest current tongues of such

Figure 9.2   Logs, undercut banks, and weed beds deflect current and provide important cover in meadow streams.

spots typically ruin across-stream presentations by moving part of your leader downstream enough ahead of the fly to cause drag. Where this happens you learn to angle your cast more downstream than across.

This form of fly fishing has particular appeal to experienced flyrodders because it provides continually changing challenges that test one's knowledge and skill. Consistent success depends on a careful approach, a basic knowledge of aquatic entomology, the ability to select fly patterns that effectively imitate specific insects, and the ability to hook and play big, wary trout on delicate tackle. In short, attention to detail is critical in almost every dimension of the endeavor.

Rigging Adaptations

At times you will want to be able to reach fish that are 50 feet or more away, perhaps due to the width of a particular stream or to the fact that you and the trout are facing one another as you cast toward the fish from upstream. Though your general-purpose rod and number 6 DT fly line may do a satisfactory job in this situation, an increasing number of meadow-stream anglers are using delicate-feeling, long graphite rods. A 9- to 9-1/2-foot graphite that casts a number 4 or 5 line may already be the standard on such streams.

The action you prefer in such a rod may be related to a specific feature or demand of this form of fishing. For example, if you have difficulty controlling your casting loops with 50 feet of line out, you could benefit from a rod that is relatively stiff throughout the butt section. On the other hand, you may prefer to have a rod that provides more shock absorption throughout its length for setting hooks and playing big fish on light tippets. This may lead you to select a rod with a little more give or flex into the butt.

If you fish this method with abbreviated double hauls you may prefer to use a weight-forward fly line. Short "tugs" or hauls with the line hand increase the speed of the line in the air and thus contribute to loop control (by shortening the time during which a line may collapse on itself). Also you will find that a weight-forward line makes it easier for you to feed or shake line out through the guides when extending a drift. (This concept will be covered in the section on Line-Handling.)

A typical leader for downstream dry fly fishing is 12 to 15 feet long with a tippet of 5X or 6X. The tippet section may be unusually long—sometimes 3 to 6 feet in length. This extra length of flexible tippet delays drag and provides extra stretch to the leader. There are times in particularly quiet, clear water when your experimentation with 7X tippets will provide enough additional action for you to make up for its lack of strength. Surprisingly big fish are taken on 6X or 7X tippets—if the material is in good condition. You should always check this by pulling on the ends of a piece of tippet material before attaching it. You become accustomed to how much pressure a new piece of tippet material should be able to withstand before breaking, and so learn to recognize when it begins to deteriorate and needs to be replaced.

This strong new tippet material (e.g., Aeon or Sussex brands) holds better with the surgeon's knot than with the traditional blood knot. Additional strength can also be achieved at the fly itself by using a variation of the clinch knot in which the tag end of the tippet is inserted through the hook eye twice.

The standard or traditional dry fly patterns are not always preferred on meadow streams, as too much hackle sticking down through the surface film is thought to be unrealistic in representing the indentations made by an insect's legs. Two of my favorite tying variations are the Paradun and Comparadun patterns. Of the two, the Paradun sits a little lower in the water and may be more effective when fish are feeding on various stages of mayflies that are down in the surface film (e.g., emerging nymph, spinner). On the other hand, the Comparadun is extremely durable and continues to float well after several fish have been taken in quick succession. Whatever fly pattern you select will usually be small (e.g., #14–18) to match the insects that most often drift in large numbers on meadow streams.

The Approach

"Mountain stream" anglers, when first exposed to a meadow stream, typically rig their fly rods and begin casting immediately. This can be a great mistake. Meadow streams give you the opportunity to learn by watching fish. To see trout holding among weed beds before you rig up, stay well back from shore, find an elevated bank with suitable light conditions, and don your polarized glasses and hat (with black under the brim). The most skilled anglers in some of our best meadow streams will sometimes observe for several hours until they find a trout that is large enough to offer a sufficient challenge to their skills. They choose not to fish the water, preferring to spend their time casting to one, visible trout.

If there is a single moment that captivated most of us to fly fishing, it was probably the moment that provided our first glimpse of a rising trout. Fly fishing writers love to categorize the various ways that a trout rises to the surface and then offer strategies to help select the correct fly for each situation. In chapter 12 of this book, I follow suit and offer my sequence for solving problems posed by selective, surface-feeding trout.

When you have watched enough to analyze the situation, it is time to rig up and move quietly to a spot well upstream of the fish. You should also resist the "mountain stream" angler's tendency to wade, unless it is necessary to get the particular drift

Figure 9.3 The quiet clarity of meadow streams permits the opportunity to study a trout's feeding tendencies before wetting a line. Remain well back from the bank when walking such streams to avoid disturbing fish and your fellow angler.

you want. The higher position on the bank affords a better view of your drifting fly and leader and any drag problems that might develop. If you have to wade, check to make sure your movements are slow enough that you can't see water being pushed ahead of you. Differences in water pressure are transmitted far and quickly in quiet, unbroken water.

As you move toward your trout from well upstream and off to one side, you should be aware of the trout's "window" or "cone of vision," which is explained in Marinaro's *In the Ring of the Rise* and Goddard and Clarke's *The Trout and the Fly*. Present the fly a few feet directly upstream of this window, so it arrives ahead of the leader. The location of the window is important because it marks the spot from which the trout can view objects above the water's surface. Your own silhouette must be low

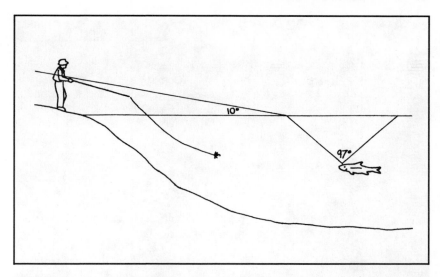

Figure 9.4 The trout's "window" to life above water leaves you 10 degrees within which to conceal yourself.

enough to fit within the first 10 degrees above horizontal (surface of the water), if you wish to remain concealed. Perhaps when descending a steep trail above a stream, you have already been impressed with how well a trout can detect your movements through clear, undisturbed water.

Casting Techniques

Trout that feed in quiet water are frequently spooked by fly lines moving back and forth through the air above them. Sometimes you will need to angle your false casts well off to one side of the fish when extending line.

Among the most useful specialized casts in this type of fishing is an old technique that has recently been popularized as the "reach cast." This cast enables you to place the fly line on the water at a different angle than with a standard, overhead cast. Its most common application is in placing the line farther upstream on the water—as if cast by someone standing several feet to your upstream side. This effect is accomplished by moving your cast-

Figure 9.5 Completing the reach cast with rod extended to the upstream side has positioned the line well upstream of a fly being drifted off to the left.

ing hand and the fly rod steadily off to one side after you have applied the initial power to the forward cast.

You begin fishing this cast with your fly rod and arm "reached" upstream. Throughout the drift, the tip is moved steadily downstream to allow the line and fly to drift naturally until the tip is "reached" downstream before lifting the fly off the water. This movement of the rod tip extends the drag-free drift.

A line that is cast down and across stream falls to the water, moves away from you, straightens, and in so doing, makes your fly drag unnaturally. The fact that this can all happen within a very few seconds underlines the need for slack in your line to delay the onset of drag. Most downstream dry fly anglers develop several slack-line casts for different situations.

Perhaps the most useful one is a cast known variously as the "bounce cast," "bump cast," or "dry fly shock cast." This cast is used when you want to put slack in the leader and line closest to the fly. Such slack keeps your fly from picking up instant drag

Figure 9.6   Side-to-side movements of the rod during the serpentine cast put ''S'' curves in the airborne line.

on across-stream presentations onto currents moving at different speeds.

This leader slack is achieved by aiming the forward cast slightly upward, overpowering it, and making a high, abrupt stop. The overpowered line is ''shocked'' as it straightens above the water, and the leader recoils or bounces back toward the line. At this time the rod tip is dropped so the line falls to the water before any of the slack can be lost.

At other times the slack is intentionally put into the line itself. In general, this works best when casting more downstream than across stream. The serpentine or ''S'' cast is the most common example. The cast is aimed high, and the rod tip moved from side to side throughout the delivery so the line falls to the water in alternating curves. I find the draw-back cast to be a more useful variation for putting slack in the line. Drawing the fly rod back toward you before the fly hits the water produces slack in the line near the fly rod. This slack becomes available for extending the drift. If your fly is cast beyond a trout's feeding lane, you

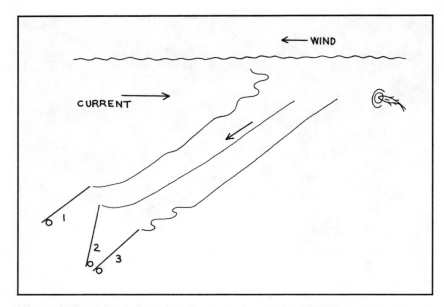

Figure 9.7 Adjusting the fly on the water: (1) When the wind has caused your fly to land upstream of the leader, (2) try raising your rod tip to draw the fly toward you until it is downstream of the tippet. (3)Then drop the tip again to allow the slack line to feed back into the drift.

can draw it back onto the water directly upstream of the trout's lie. This feature makes the cast popular with boat guides, who are paid to produce fish for some rather inept casters.

The best slack-line casts for particular pools are sometimes combinations of basic techniques. My favorite is one that Frank Collin and I put together one August day on Hat Creek, the popular meadow stream near Burney, California.

We were trying to get as long a drag-free drift as possible in slow water beyond the fast currents our line had to drift in. Our best drifts were achieved by combining five elements: (a) extra long tippets (5 to 6 feet); (b) low back cast and high forward "pile cast"; (c) release of line during the forward cast; (d) early dropping of the rod tip; and (e) a mending of the line before the fly hit the water. We laughingly refer to this particular combination as a "Ray Guy" cast because the fly has a five-second "hang time" in the air, like so many of the famous punter's best kicks.

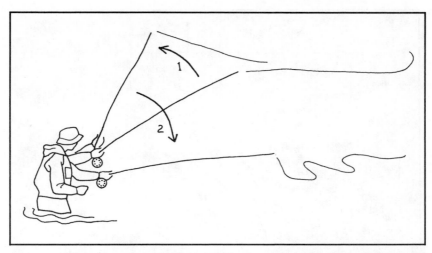

Figure 9.8 Slack line on the water near the rod is achieved with a draw-back cast. As the line straightens in the air on your forward cast, pull the rod (and the line) back toward you (1). Then drop the rod tip low (2) to place the slack on the water. In a downstream presentation, the fly can drift naturally until the last of this slack line has straightened.

Line-Handling and Fishing Techniques

One of the fascinating things about this kind of fishing is analyzing currents to decide what adjustments to make in casting position, cast, and line-handling to achieve a drag-free drift.

A common error people make, in my estimation, is to cast over the fish without first checking the drift and making some adjustments. I see people put down trout with their very first presentation because of unanticipated drag. Often they are fishing a much longer cast than the situation requires. Some years back, André Puyans, the internationally known fly fisherman and fly tyer, introduced me to the concept of an "imaginary grid" on the surface of the water. This envisioned grid is an aid in remembering to move your fly systematically closer to the fish with each cast. Your first casts should fall far short of the fish—too short to draw strikes or rejections. However, they enable you to observe the way your fly is drifting. As you cast the fly closer to the fish, you are making adjustments in casting angle, line length, and

Figure 9.9   The loop of line to be fed into this downstream drift is visible dropping to the water just in front of the angler.

type of cast until you are satisfied with the drift. Then, instead of extending more line, your final adjustments onto the fish are made by moving closer to it (when conditions permit). So your own position, rather than line length, is varied when finally moving "on to the fish."

I recall a day that seemed to offer ideal conditions for the use of this technique. A good brown trout had risen tight against the grassy bank in a meadow section of the famed Madison River. As I was testing the drift with my fly still a good 6 feet out from the bank, the "sophisticated bank feeder" did the unexpected and moved out to take my fly. Totally unprepared for that possibility, I missed the fish. I hadn't moved my fly close enough to consider that I was fishing it yet. Sometimes trout just won't follow the scripts we prepare for them.

A common form of line-handling on many meadow streams is "feeding" line into the drift. Feeding a controlled amount of

Figure 9.10   An up-and-down flip of the rod tip has taken some of this line out through the fly rod where it will prolong the fly's drag-free float.

line extends the drift to fish that are exceptionally wary or simply beyond casting range downstream. To move such additional line out through your fly rod after the cast, you must first make sure that line is available by pulling it off your reel. Then, after lowering your rod tip close to the water, you flip it up and down when feeding line. More precisely, you feed line out during the upward flip of the tip. Flipping the tip upward lifts a little line off the water and starts it moving away from you. Any line you let slip out through your line hand during this time will follow right along behind and settle to the water beyond your rod tip which is being lowered again. This technique, which can be practiced on even a small lawn, works best with a weight-forward line.

Of course if the fly is refused, it must then be brought back toward you without pulling the line, leader, and fly over the fish. To do this you move the rod to the side away from the trout. This procedure consumes time and soaks the fly. If I must feed

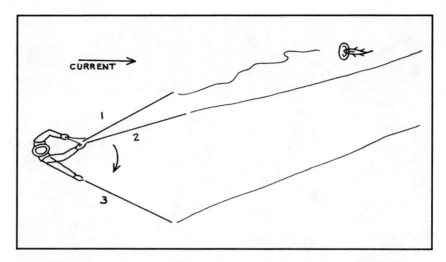

Figure 9.11   Top view of an angler (1) making a downstream presentation to a working fish, (2) facing the problem of returning the extended line upstream without disturbing his quarry, and (3) solving the problem by tipping the rod off to the opposite side to strip in line.

line in this way and want to watch my fly for drag, I first select a buoyant pattern, such as a small Horner Deer Hair or Comparadun, and hope it does the job of attracting fish.

Mending line also has a place in downstream dry fly fishing, though some anglers believe you can't mend without also moving your fly. Most commonly I use the mend when the line close to me is drifting much faster than the fly itself farther out. If you use a long leader and your fly has been drifting a couple of seconds it is not difficult to mend line without moving the fly. And several mends might be required to achieve the drift you want.

Hooking and Landing the Fish

Successfully hooking a trout that is downstream of you can be a tricky business. In effect, you are pulling the fly back upstream, out of the fish's mouth, rather than setting it into the side of the jaw as you often do when downstream of the fish. The combination of fine tippets, small hooks, and very large trout can result in many fish being lost at the moment of the take.

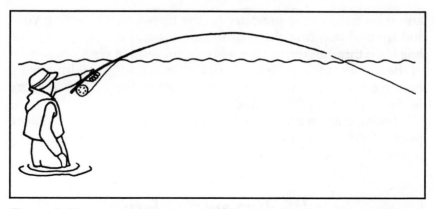

Figure 9.12 Minimizing resistance against a running fish means holding the rod high (to keep line off the water) and horizontal (to let line slip through the guides).

As indicated previously, you may want to select a fly rod with this moment in mind, choosing one that is soft enough to be forgiving when excessive force is applied in reaction to a sudden strike.

Sometimes a trout takes your fly when the line is on the water in a long curve. If you set the hook by raising the rod in this situation, you encounter considerable resistance of surface tension on your line. Your movement will be transmitted to the fly quicker by moving your rod sideways away from your fly line.

However, when the line on the water is relatively straight, you should set the hook by raising the rod rather than pulling it back or to either side. Since it is easy to break fish off at this time, you should hold the line loosely enough so that some of it can slip through your fingers as you raise the rod. I find that I am most likely to break fish off on the strike if (a) I have lost vision of my fly, (b) I am fishing an unusually long line, or (c) the rise comes unexpectedly.

In playing a fish that is pulling downstream away from you, your main concern should be to minimize the pressure or resistance against it and your tippet. (When the fish stops using energy, then is the time for you to increase pressure.) One thing you can do is to hold your rod high to keep as much line in the air as possible, since line on the water increases the resistance and thus adds to the pressure on the tippet. But lowering your rod tip and pointing the rod directly toward the fish helps the line slide through the guides with a minimum of resistance. Both of these concepts can be incorporated into a single technique by holding the rod hand high, but keeping the rod in a more horizontal than vertical angle.

I realize there are times when you will want to apply more pressure to a downstream-pulling fish, such as when you can't follow it farther downstream.

Wading and Safety

Even when not wading, safety should be on your mind. In walking the bank of a meadow stream, you should anticipate the presence of undercut banks whenever the main current is on your side, and expect beaver or muskrat tunnels to be underfoot. The high grass on the banks of these streams often conceals holes or soft footing. These are all reasons for walking carefully and testing the footing constantly. It is not a place to be in a hurry.

Variations of This Method

Although not discussed here, many dry fly anglers fish downstream angles on the mixed currents of mountain streams. Leonard Wright's variation of twitching the downstream-cast dry fly to imitate the upstream surge of an egg-laying caddisfly is a specialized application of this general method.

Selected Readings

Arbona, F. (1980). *Mayflies, the angler and the trout*. Tulsa, OK: Winchester Press.

Caucci, A., & Nastasi, B. (1975). *Hatches*. Woodside, NY: Comparahatch.

Cutter, R. (1984). Down current presentation. In Scientific Anglers (Ed.), *Fly fishing handbook*. Point Pleasant, NJ: Aqua-Field.

Harrop, R. (1980). Meadow streams—The ultimate challenge. In Scientific Anglers (Ed.), *Fly fishing handbook*. Point Pleasant, NJ: Aqua–Field.

Harrop, R. (1984, July). The final inch. *Fly Fisherman*.

Marinaro, V. (1976). *In the ring of the rise*. New York: Crown.

Proper, D.C. (1982). *What the trout said*. New York: Alfred A. Knopf.

Robins, K. (1979, Fall). Nymph or dun. *The flyfisher*.

Swisher, D., & Richards, C. (1980). *Tying the Swisher/Richards Flies*. Harrisburg, PA: Stackpole.

Wright, L. (1972). *Fishing the dry fly as a living insect*. New York: Dutton.

10
Chapter

Upstream Nymphing: Further Challenges in Line Control, Naturalness, and Depth

One of my greatest pleasures in fly fishing is experimenting with different techniques or variations. Yet, if I had to limit myself to one method, there would be no hesitation in making my choice. I would fish a nymph with the line laid out on the water upstream of me. In some respects this type of fishing is an extension of the short-line, sunken-fly method described earlier. It is different in that there is more line being fished, and that the leader butt is floating on the water rather than cutting directly through it.

This upstream method of nymphing owes part of its appeal to the fact that it is also similar to upstream, dry fly fishing, at least in the approach, the casting, and much of the line-handling. It has long been recognized as the most palatable alternative for the dry fly angler who is forced to sink the fly to attract trout. I had to learn from experience that some of the best fish in moving

Figure 10.1 Adapting nymphing techniques to the variety of pools and runs found in mountain streams is part of the challenge of fishing such water effectively.

water seldom feed near the surface. I mentally kick myself every time I think of how many decent-sized trout I fished over unknowingly during the 1940s and 50s—when I fished only with dry flies.

For me, much of the pleasure in this method is in the subtlety of strike detection, particularly when the first indication of a trout's take is something less than an obvious dip, jerk, or stop in my leader. Maintaining enough line control to detect at least some of the subtle takes in various types of water is challenge enough for any angler.

The adaptability of upstream nymphing to many different types of water also adds to the appeal of this method. The terminal rigging, in particular, can be altered in a number of ways to accommodate the need for line control, depth, and naturalness in stretches of water that are quite different from one another.

The earliest application of this method may have been in gently flowing streams of England. In a book published in 1939, *Nymph*

Fishing for Chalk Stream Trout, Skues recounted how he started using this method to stalk individual, visible trout years before. This method is equally effective in a wide assortment of mountain-stream riffles and pools, where "fishing the water" makes more sense.

This type of fishing seems least appropriate in very fast runs (e.g., rapids, fast riffles, and glides) and in very short runs (e.g., cascades, pocket water). I have already described methods that are better suited to such water.

Rigging Adaptations

Fly rods used for upstream nymphing are as varied as the water itself. Where the method is used to cast substantial weight in rough water, you may want a rod that casts a number 7 line, but where it is used to cast small nymphs in quiet flow, you may prefer one that casts a number 4 or 5 line. Our general-purpose rod will suffice in either situation.

Though I own a few sink-tip lines, I invariably use floating lines in this method. If I am casting much terminal weight (e.g., one or two number 7 split shot) a distance of up to 50 feet, I use a double-tapered line rather than a weight-forward. The extra weight in the larger diameter behind the first 30 feet handles the casting of leader weight better than the thinner weight-forward line.

As I have stated, much of the adaptability of this method comes through adjusting the terminal tackle to "match the water." This may be done by varying (a) the length and tippet diameter of the leader, (b) the placement and quantity of leader weight, (c) the type and placement of a "strike indicator" (if used), and (d) the number, weight, size, and pattern of flies. With so many possible ways of adjusting your rigging, it's no wonder it takes years of experience to accumulate enough trial-and-error learning to become truly versatile in nymphing.

It might be of value here to describe several of the most distinctive riggings that are used in upstream nymphing. First, the one that is most similar to dry fly fishing involves little more than replacing the dry fly with a lightly weighted nymph. The leader butt is usually greased with flotant to facilitate strike detection in the shallow, quiet pools where this variation is typically used.

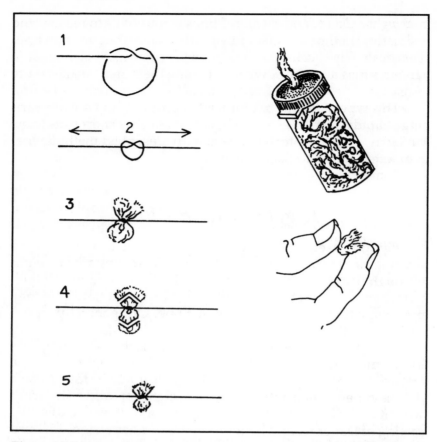

Figure 10.2   An indicator may be nothing more than a piece of bright-colored yarn placed on your leader and trimmed to a round shape.

In my teaching, I have noticed that some experienced dry fly anglers have difficulty shifting their concentration from a fly they can no longer see (but still look for) to the visible part of the leader. The addition of a more obvious ''strike indicator'' serves to focus their attention while they become accustomed to this method. Though a wide variety of materials are used for this fly fisher's ''bobber,'' I most often attach to my leader a small red piece of the best floating synthetic yarn I can get my hands on, trimming it into a small ball of about 1/8 of an inch in diameter. My favorite way of inserting this yarn onto my leader is to form two loops in such a way that they become a Clove Hitch when doubled and tightened around the yarn. Should you wish to remove the indicator, it is an easy matter to pull the yarn out and then back the Clove Hitch off.

Near dark I have been known to use an Elk Hair Caddis as my indicator. I first resorted to this tactic one evening after having several trout grab my pink indicator instead of my olive-brown nymph. I reasoned that if the trout were that determined to make me look bad, they were at least going to find a hook in the indicator. (We anglers have wonderful personalities.)

Some evening, when you're fishing a visible dry fly and want to add to your fun, attach an extra piece of tippet material a couple of feet long to the eye of your fly. Then tie a nymph onto the other end of this tippet material. I'm sometimes surprised which fly outfishes the other.

Usually I prefer not to use an indicator when nymphing. In fact I have seen even a small indicator spook fish on more than one occasion. However, an indicator is a useful crutch when visibility becomes difficult due to glare, shade, or chop on the water's surface.

In quiet water, the placement of the indicator becomes critical, because the trout often pick up the nymph without moving very far or very fast. To detect such quiet takes, the indicator must be as close to the fly as possible while still providing enough tippet length to get the fly down near the trout's feeding level. This is accomplished with a rather vertical drop of the fly, using as much weight as you can without sinking the indicator. California guide Bob Howe introduced me to this concept of indicator fishing some years back. Bob, Dave Hickson, and Dean Schubert have done more to fine-tune this particular form of indicator fishing than anyone I am aware of. Their techniques are described in the May 1986 issue of *Fly Fisherman* magazine.

A very different rigging may be called for on big, freestone streams where depth and current speed vary considerably from pool to pool. The most extreme adjustments are made by changing leader length. This can be done quickly when the leader butt has been connected to the tippet by loops, as publicized by Lefty Kreh. In my particular adaptation of this loop system, the permanent leader butt is 5 feet long, and my pre-tied tippets allow me to fish leaders from 6-1/2 to 15 feet in length. With the interconnecting loops, the only knots you need to tie on the stream are those at the fly itself.

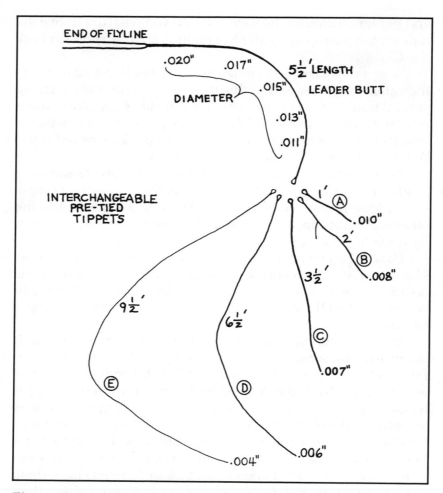

Figure 10.3 Changing leader lengths and tippet diameters quickly on the stream can be accomplished by using a "loop system." A surgeon's loop tied at the end of a "permanent" tapered leader butt can be connected and disconnected quickly with similar loops tied at the thick ends of various tippets. These tippets are tied, packaged, and labeled before fishing and carried in a leader wallet.

Most of the time, however, such extreme changes in leader length are not necessary, and you can stay with a leader of about nine feet. One much shorter than this sometimes gets the fly too close to the line on upstream casts or fails to give you adequate depth from the floating line. A leader much longer than

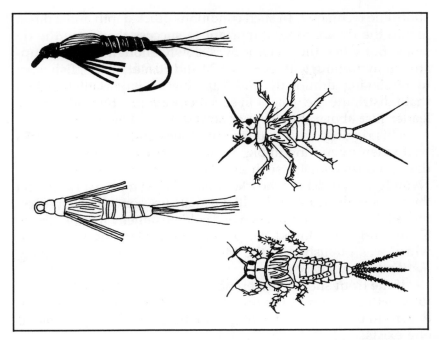

Figure 10.4   ''Realism'' in fly patterns gains importance in quiet water where trout have time to inspect their food. André Puyan's AP nymphs are realistic enough to imitate mayfly nymphs in slow water yet general enough to pass for either stonefly nymphs (top) or mayfly nymphs (bottom) where currents are faster. The distinguishing feature between these two nymphs is the presence of gills on the mayfly's abdomen.

nine feet becomes more difficult to cast with weight (particularly when trees line the banks) and is more difficult to control in the water where currents are mixed. When fishing this leader, you can adjust to variations in depth and current speed by changing the size or number of removable split shot on the leader. The quickness with which this form of leader weight can be added or removed is its most important characteristic, because you might need to change weight two or three times in the same run.

The exact placement of the weight may have a pronounced effect on how naturally your fly sinks, and how many strikes come while it is sinking. When all the weight is concentrated in one place, such as in a single, weighted fly, that weight plummets to the bottom with little, if any, appeal to the trout. Yet in fast riffle water, a single, heavy fly fishes well, particularly with a short-line technique. In such conditions quick depth and a direct feel to the fly are more important to success than how the fly sinks. But when the water moves slowly enough to permit upstream nymphing with between 20 and 50 feet of line, fish react to the sinking, drifting fly, and naturalness is important. It is then that I distribute the weight in several locations—typically on the leader just above the dropper strand as well as on the flies.

This rigging, with two weighted flies and split shot, works well when nymphing in big, mountain streams. Flies we have discussed previously, such as a Leisenring Spider, Hare's Ear Nymph, Gray-Hackle Peacock, or dark AP Nymph, work well on the dropper fly in about size 10. I usually use something larger on the tail fly, such as a number 6 or 8 golden-stonefly nymph. Frank Collin and I developed the pattern we prefer, the CK Perlid, which was published in the May-June 1981 issue of *Flyfishing the West* (now *Flyfishing*).

If the trout show a preference for one fly, I switch the other for a pattern closer to the one that is working. In this way I try to zero in on a specific feeding tendency as early as possible, if one exists.

I recall a day in which Dick Holland took two 15-inch brown trout in quick succession from the same spot on a small meadow stream. He found that the fish that had inhaled his scud imitation had been feeding strictly on scuds, while the one that had grabbed the caddis larva on his dropper was gorging on caddis larvae. It was as if these two trout had made a pact to survive by dividing up the available food rather than competing directly for the same items. Charles Brooks told a similar story of two nice trout that were taken during the same hour from a cove in Montana's Hebgen Lake. One had been selective to dragonfly nymphs, while the other had dined exclusively on midge pupae.

How do we know when fish are going to partition the available food in this way and how often it happens? I don't believe that any of our fly fishing experts have nearly enough knowledge of the changing variables of the trout's world to consistently predict such feeding tendencies—especially when fishing an unfamiliar piece of water. And frankly, I'm glad they don't. To me, the knowledge that some bottom-living trout do feed specifically at times is reason enough to start a day's nymphing with two quite different flies on my leader.

The Approach

When "fishing the water" with this method, your approach is basically the same as when fishing up and across stream with a dry fly. Again, you position yourself where you are best able to lay the line and fly on relatively even-flowing water. Concealment is not as critical, however, when fishing to bottom-holding trout under a turbulent water surface.

When conditions permit you to spot an individual trout, you spend a few moments observing its feeding behavior before attempting the first cast. In such gentle flow, you may want to position yourself to cast as much across stream as upstream in order to see the trout as clearly as possible when the fly approaches it.

The most fascinating part of the approach is looking at the water to decide how you will fish it. The more experienced and versatile you are, the more options you have. Sometimes, I force myself to "read the water" out loud—where the currents converge, where there is cover, where the fish should be, what is unusual. By doing this I often become aware of something subtle that I would have overlooked by reading the water unconsciously. This is important late in the season when hordes of anglers have worked over the obvious spots. Then you should read the water for something the others have missed, approach it from a different side, or use a different fishing technique.

Casting Techniques

Some of the casts I have mentioned previously, including the reach, roll, and curve casts, can be used when terminal weight isn't excessive. Casting problems arise when split shot or heavy flies are needed to achieve depth in rough water. You have already been advised to use large loops to cast weight safely. Even then, I find that most people who are relatively new to the sport don't have the experienced timing to control a cast with heavy split shot and are well advised to use less weight initially. Then weight can be added gradually as you become familiar with the different feel of this type of casting stroke.

One casting variation that is useful whether leader weight is applied or not is the "off-side cast" alluded to in other chapters.

Figure 10.5   Lowered left hip and outward-thrust elbow help tilt the rod for an off-side cast. Though the line has passed on the angler's left, note that the casting hand stays on his right.

This is the cast where you try to move the fly and line back and forth on your noncasting side (your left side, if a right-handed caster). In wadable freestone rivers, the streamside alders or willows may force you to spend much of the day using this technique, which is sometimes referred to as casting "off your left shoulder" or the "tilted plane cast." Mel Krieger has used these terms rather than "backhand cast" because it is a different technique. Mel stresses keeping your casting hand on the right side, where it can apply power most effectively, whereas the backhand cast brings the casting hand over to the left side of your body. Mel prefers to tip or cant the rod to his left side by rotating the palm of his casting hand forward. My preference is to cant the rod by moving my elbow away from my side, thus keeping my forearm aligned with the canted rod. Both methods work, so you might experiment to find which you prefer.

This power emphasis becomes extremely important if you use the cast as I do in delivering split shot 45 feet or more upstream on the off-side. With experienced timing and a wide arc, the fly can

Figure 10.6 Cast completed, the angler prepares to fish a drift close to a protected lie. Overpowering the next off-side cast would produce a curve around the upstream side of the rock.

be dropped with surprisingly little splash. Many anglers don't realize that 45 feet of fly line represents enough weight to sharply reduce any disruptive effect that leader weight has on casting.

If you don't trust yourself with the off-side cast, you can always resort to the old technique of turning to face downstream, and reversing the casting strokes. In other words, you direct a forward cast downstream (as your back cast) and then deliver the fly upstream and onto the water with a back cast (used as your forward cast). This technique eliminates the need to cast off your left side, especially when learning to handle terminal weight. This technique is also useful when a wind blows hard from your casting side as it often does on lakes. One such day on Pyramid Lake in Nevada, I caught a seven pound cutthroat with this cast.

Split shot becomes more difficult to cast when less line is used. It may become necessary to use the tension cast described in chapter 5, where the friction of the water bends the rod to deliver the line upstream safely. The roll cast can also be used

Figure 10.7 The line has drifted downstream to our left and forced this angler to move the rod tip to that side of his body to continue roll casting.

Figure 10.8 Reversing the casting strokes: The tree on the picture's right has prevented this angler from making a long upstream cast (toward the camera). So he has turned his back to his target and uses a forward casting motion to make his back cast (away from the camera).

Figure 10.9 The angler completes the cast by using a back casting motion to present the fly back upstream to our left. He is about to pivot toward us to face his fly as it drifts back to him.

effectively with split shot as long as the leader weight is near the surface when the cast is made.

Line-Handling and Fishing Techniques

The interplay between depth, naturalness, and line control sometimes means one is emphasized at the expense of another. Each pool is different, and the first few drifts will tell you if adjustments are needed to provide additional depth or perhaps better line control. Sometimes such adjustments can be made by varying the cast to present the fly and leader differently, without having to make alterations in your rigging.

If, for example, you need more depth early in the drift, you could use a tuck cast as mentioned in chapter 7, or use any casting variation that puts slack in your leader. When you use a fine tippet and present it in loose coils, resistance to the fly's sinking is at a minimum.

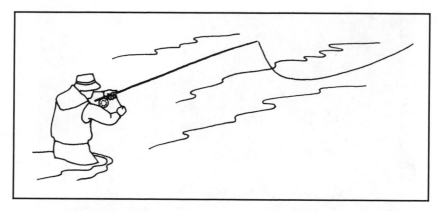

Figure 10.10   Constant stripping of line becomes a way of life for those who nymph upstream in fast water.

However, there are other times when control of the line be-comes more important than depth or naturalness. You need a drift that starts with as straight a leader as possible if the trout are hitting early in the drift, or tentatively in general, or when the submerged leader is developing excessive slack during the drift. A well-executed roll cast is one way of achieving this presentation with very little splash near the fly.

After the cast, the rod is sometimes manipulated for line-handling purposes. A ''roll mend'' is a useful technique when you cast a nymph up and across stream to a slot of slow water that lies beyond fast currents. As the fly begins to sink immediately after the cast, you cant the rod to the downstream side and make a sideward roll cast upstream that affects only the line that hasn't already started to sink. If done correctly, a little line rolls out and falls on the upstream side of the sinking leader. Perhaps more important is the fact that this maneuver can be repeated several times in quick succession to keep line from settling into fast currents between you and the fly. When the fly has drifted closer to you, a high rod and extended arm take over in preventing the line from falling on the fast water.

Another distinctive use of the fly rod is to fish with the rod tip held off to one side, rather than pointed upstream toward the fly. This technique is useful whenever you are standing off to the side of the water being fished and want to keep the rod tip positioned directly downcurrent of the drifting fly line. The

Figure 10.11 When standing off to one side of the water you are fishing, try to keep the rod tip directly downcurrent from the drifting fly line. The direct line between the low tip and the fly enables you to reduce slack quickly and hook more fish.

direct line between the low rod tip and the fly enables you to quickly reduce any slack that forms during the drift.

I use this variation primarily to fish deep through a narrow, fast chute of water, such as between two large midstream rocks. Some of the biggest fish I have taken from freestone streams have found a protected lie beneath a strip of fast water. Such fish get large because their hold is not visible from above and they cannot be taken by conventional fly fishing methods. They get bypassed by anglers who work the water regularly.

I fish such runs by casting almost straight upstream with more weight on the leader than usual—enough to lower the fly through fast water. Once this weight has cut through the fast currents, it becomes a liability due to its potential for hanging up on rubble or submerged snags on the stream's bottom. I try to avoid such hang-ups by stripping line in fast enough to keep the weight from settling. This means trying to keep the line and leader butt moving as horizontally as possible through the water, while watching the end of the fly line for an indication of a trout's grab.

At times you may have to move the fly slightly faster than the current, but even then the trout in such runs often take the fly decisively. This is fortunate because current speed that requires fast, long strips makes line control and strike detection difficult.

Hooking and Landing the Fish

When looking for the trout's take, I typically watch the farthest visible part of the leader (or strike indicator) for any departure whatsoever from its steady downstream movement. The subtle indication that a trout has picked up the fly is usually a change in this rate of movement of the leader. Inexperienced eyes will not see it, and it accounts for what some writers refer to as the "mystique of nymphing."

One day on California's Hot Creek, I took ten fish in an hour and a half while a stream biologist stood next to me watching my leader. He didn't detect a single strike, because none was as obvious as a sudden stop, dip, or jerk. The movement of the leader had continued, but at a changed rate. It is a detectable difference, not magic. If you are new to this form of fishing, you first learn to recognize the more obvious, sudden movements of the leader, which are usually decisive pickups by the fish.

The situation is different when you are nymphing to trout you can see. When satisfied that your nymph has been cast upstream of the trout in its feeding lane, you watch the leader (or indicator) until it approaches the fish. At this moment you shift your vision to the trout itself, which in effect, becomes your "indicator." Any turn or lift in its position or flash of a white mouth should be interpreted as a pickup. Thus you are using your indicator to keep track of the location of your nymph as it drifts unseen near the stream's bottom. As Bob Howe puts it, your indicator is being used as a "locator" in this technique.

When watching for strikes, I prefer to use short strips to keep my line hand close to the rod. Thus I leave myself a long distance

Figure 10.12   A horizontally bent rod helps steer a hooked fish away from snags or obstructions.

to pull the line when needed to remove slack in setting the hook. And, as mentioned before, I also move the rod away from the line pull.

When large split shot are used and the entire leader is submerged, the line-leader junction becomes the strike indicator. However, when any of the leader butt is visible either on or below the surface, I watch it to detect strikes because it provides an earlier and more pronounced indication. George Anderson, the respected guide and shop owner of Livingston, Montana, advocates using red monofilament for the leader butt to facilitate strike detection in this type of deep nymphing.

When playing a hooked fish, it isn't always in your best interest to hold the rod upright. When you want to lead a fish away from an obstacle or keep its head from moving freely above the surface, it pays to hold the rod to one side with a horizontal bend. In such cases I try to put pressure on whenever I can get the rod to pull from the side of the fish. Hal Janssen recommends a different strategy with big, hard-to-control trout. He likes to put pressure on the fish from the obstruction side, believing that big fish will move away from the pressure of the rod and from the obstruction. Of course, whenever weed beds are present or the fish starts running, you should return the rod to a more vertical position.

Wading and Safety

Like most anglers who wade upstream, I had to learn the hard way to plan ahead. Maybe you won't have to.

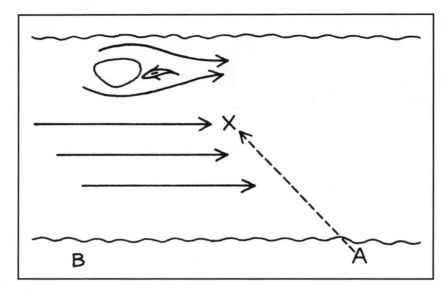

Figure 10.13   Before a tough wade, such as the one drawn from A to X, check on a safe upstream ''escape'' such as the route from X to B.

What may happen is that you spot an unusually good piece of water on the far side of the stream, and by bracing yourself against the current and carefully wading up and across the heavy water, you are able to reach it and fish. Only then do you realize you have a problem. You find there is no wadable return route except the one that brought you. Only now it involves a down and across stream wade through strong currents. You may have to continue facing upstream to keep yourself braced against the current, and painfully inch your way back downstream with what seems like a thousand backward steps. For a while, you are a prisoner of the river. The lesson you learn is if you can't see a return route before first wading into tough currents, don't go.

Variations of This Method

To some extent this chapter on upstream nymphing has been a discussion of variations. However, there is one variation that deserves special mention—a variation for big, deep, slow-moving ''bait holes.''

One spring day in the late 1960s, I was pool-testing to confirm for myself that a 6-foot leader would sink a weighted fly faster than a 10-foot leader (other things being equal). For my own convenience, I had rigged the two rods with floating lines. Indeed, I found that my moderately weighted fly sunk quicker on the shorter leader, but as I continued to watch, I saw the other fly eventually overtake it and sink deeper yet. I began to think of floating lines, long leaders, and slow, deep pools.

A week later, I had the opportunity to watch someone fish who had already put this "program" or fishing variation together. Dick Holland, who has a reputation for taking exceptionally large fish from heavily fished waters, took ten fish between 14 and 24 inches using this method while the local fly fishing expert was doing well to catch that number in pocket water—but all under 14 inches. From that day forward, the trout I have taken from certain big freestone streams are larger on the average than those I took previously.

In this variation you use as long a leader as necessary to get to the bottom and as much leader and fly weight as necessary to achieve a slow, natural drift. Often you fish along the shoreline because the water is too deep to wade. The fly is cast well upstream and fished carefully from the moment it lands. By the time it has approached you, the leader is dropping vertically from the line-leader junction which is held at the surface. Once again, any change in the rate of the leader's drift is likely to mean fish—often big, soft-hitting trout that wouldn't be felt on a sinking line.

Selected Readings

Anderson, G. (1984). Four deadly nymphing tricks. In Scientific Anglers (Ed.), *Fly fishing handbook*. Point Pleasant, NJ: Aqua-Field.

Collin, F., & Kyte, A. (1981). CK Perlid—The rolling stone. *Fly-fishing the West*, **4**(2), 22–25.

Fothergill, C. (1970, February). Nymphing the roaring fork. *Fly Fisherman*.

Fothergill, C. (1979, Season Opener). Nymphing with weight. *Fly Fisherman*.

Goddard, J., & Clark, B. (1980). *The trout and the fly*. Garden City, NY: Doubleday.

Hickson, D., & Schubert, D. (1986, May). Dead drift nymphing. *Fly Fisherman*.

Kreh, L. (1979, Early Season). Using the loop knot for tippets. *Fly Fisherman*.

Krieger, M. (1981, March). The tilted–plane cast. *Fly Fisherman*.

Kyte, A. (1981, March). Nymph fishing: The "match the water" techniques. *Field & Stream*.

Mingo, J. (1980, Late Season). Floating nymphs on spring creeks. *Fly Fisherman*.

Puyans, A. (1975, May/June). Tying the A.P. nymph series. *Angler*.

Sawyer, F. (1973). *Nymphs and the trout*. New York: Crown.

Skues, G.E.M. (1939). *Nymph fishing for chalk stream trout*. London: A. & C. Black.

Whitlock, D. (1972, August). Nymphs in "trouble waters." *Outdoor Life*.

A Deep-Nymph, Floating Line Method for Lakes: Sensitivity and Depth in Still Water

T oward the end of the previous chapter I described a variation for nymphing deep in moving water with a floating line. A similar concept is gaining popularity in still water, particularly in lakes with extensive weed beds or bottoms that harbor large numbers of small aquatic animals. The invertebrates—midge larvae and pupae, mayfly nymphs, water boatmen, and small crustaceans (scud)—are frequently vulnerable in large enough numbers that trout can feed while cruising deep, without having to make energy-expending rushes.

Based on this type of deep-feeding behavior, fly fishermen such as Brian Clarke of England and Hal Janssen of California have spent years refining concepts that have led to a still water method of fishing small, slow-moving nymphs with a floating line. This floating line method features light, sensitive equipment and the imitation of small, aquatic insects, both of which contribute

Figure 11.1   A floating line and long leader provide an enjoyable and effective way to reach fish that feed deep on small, still water invertebrates.

to its appeal to fly fishing anglers. When trout are feeding leisurely on small invertebrates, this floating line concept is preferred to sinking line lake methods (described in chapter 6), because the soft takes are transmitted to the surface far more readily along a light, thin leader than along a thick, heavy fly line. By contrast, sinking line methods sometimes seem little more than dredging the bottom with large Woolly-Worms.

This floating line lake method, more than any other, is distinctive for its blending of sensitivity and depth.

Though the floating line concept has some attractive features, it would be a mistake to leave your sinking lines at home. They may be needed should a strong wind come up unexpectedly and push your floating line along the surface so as to interfere with your drift (and ability to detect strikes). And there's always the possibility that the trout will change their feeding pattern, necessitating your switch to a fast sinking line and a different fly, such as a leech pattern.

Rigging Adaptations

The link between a floating line and a nymph fished from between 5 and 15 feet deep is a very long leader, usually between 15 and 25 feet in length. A leader of this length can be difficult for inexperienced anglers to cast and requires a well-designed fly rod. In fact this form of fly fishing places more demands than any other on the term "general-purpose fly rod." On one hand, the rod used here must be sufficiently stiff to deliver a fly attached to the longest of leaders, and yet be sufficiently soft to protect the lightest of tippets against savage grabs by big fish.

The need for softness is met in part by selecting lightweight fly lines; most anglers use lines in the 3- to 5-weight range when fishing this method. In addition to being concerned about the weight of their fly line, these anglers are also concerned about the effect of its color.

John Goddard is a quiet-water specialist from England who believes that the flash of a light-colored fly line overhead spooks trout in clear water below. Hal Janssen likes dark red because the dark shade minimizes this overhead flash while the red color is visible on the water. He advocates dying your fly line to get the proper color.

I tie up my own knotted leaders for this method based on a "leader formula" developed by Hal Janssen. His tippets are long and fine, often down to 7X, so there is little restraint to the sinking of the fly. When I first tested one of his leaders, I was amazed how fast a size 16 weighted PT nymph can sink through the first few feet of still water.

For those of you who tie your own leaders, Hal's basic building block is his leader butt. As he works down in diameter size, each successive piece of monofilament is two-thirds the length of the previous piece. When he has added a section that is only 10 to 12 inches long, he continues to add sections of this length until he has worked down to the diameter he wants for his long tippet section. I feel there is a basic logic to this concept in terms

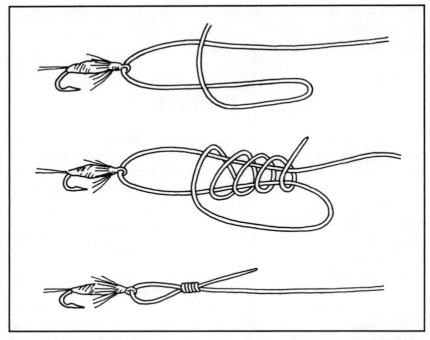

Figure 11.2 The slip-knot feature of the Duncan's loop or uni knot allows you to fish nymphs with a little extra swimming action.

of the transmission of energy from one piece to another. At any rate I like the way his leaders turn over.

With tippets in the 7X range and the possibility of large, strong trout, your terminal knots should be strong. I have already mentioned the variation of the clinch knot in which the end of the tippet is inserted twice through the eye of the hook. Some quiet water nymphers prefer a different knot, the Duncan's loop. Its slip-knot feature is thought to give the nymph a little extra "swimming action" as well as to provide shock absorption when the fish hits.

Anglers who fish this method are anything but casual practitioners of the sport. I would be surprised to find one who didn't possess an assortment of fly patterns that specifically imitate many of the common invertebrates that inhabit lakes. However, a good initial pattern is a small, weighted, light-toned nymph such as a size 14 or 16 Hare's-Ear Nymph, Otter Shrimp, or any

Figure 11.3   The impressionistic qualities of the Zug Bug (top) and Hare's-Ear nymphs contribute to their effectiveness in representing a variety of small, aquatic invertebrates.

olive mayfly nymph. These patterns could suggest scuds, water boatmen, caddis pupae, light-toned mayfly nymphs, midge pupae, or small dragonfly nymphs. A second selection might be something like a size 16 Sawyer's PT nymph or a Zug Bug to pass as a dark mayfly nymph, cased caddis larva, or midge larva. Two specific patterns worth including due to their importance as trout food in many lakes are (a) midge pupa (e.g., size 16 to 20), and (b) damselfly nymph (i.e., size 10 to 14).

The color of the natural insect in lakes is often that of the background, whether it is aquatic vegetation or lake bottom. If a second trip is planned to the lake you are fishing, you may want to collect and photograph insects (before true color fades) in order to return with more realistic imitations of the trout's food.

When fishing deep your nymphs should be wrapped with anywhere from 4 to 10 turns of 1-amp lead wire. In fact, having some with four turns and others with 10 enables you to vary the depths you fish without altering your leader length.

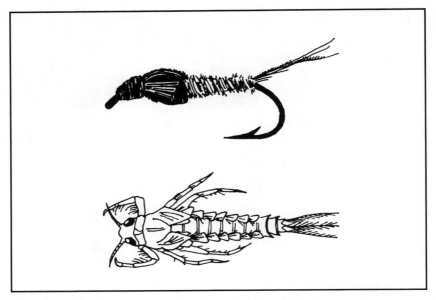

Figure 11.4   The slender silhouette of swimming mayfly nymphs suggests the use of Frank Sawyer's PT nymph. Compare the swept-back legs of this quiet-water insect with the sturdy legs of the crawling mayfly nymphs in figure 10.4.

The Approach

This type of fishing can be done from a boat or float tube, while walking the banks, or while wading a shoreline. When wading, you should stalk the fish carefully, placing casts alongside shallow weed beds and over the tops of those that lie deeper. Much of the previously covered material that dealt with approaching trout in lakes continues to hold true in this type of fishing.

In the absence of visible feeders, you often try to fish close to the bottom. The depth to fish can sometimes be estimated by studying the slope of the land above the waterline.

Casting Techniques

One of the most difficult things about casting a 20-foot leader is getting your fly out onto the water in the first place, especially if you happen to be standing in knee-high grass. Brian Clarke's

Figure 11.5   When stalking fish among weed beds, try to disturb the water as little as possible.

writing alerted me to a technique that alleviates this problem. Before attempting to cast, you pull fly line off the reel until you have a couple of yards of it beyond the rod tip. Then you pick up the fly rod in your casting hand and grasp the fly in your other hand. As you begin to cast, you continue to hold onto the fly until the line and leader have cleared the grass and are moving back and forth with the movement of the rod. Then, on the next forward cast, release the fly, which should land on the water in front of you.

I use fewer casting variations with this method than with any other. It is probably because I need a well-executed overhead cast

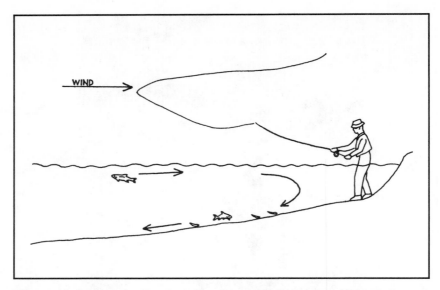

Figure 11.6 On a windy day, lake water moves and concentrates food along the leeward shore. Casting into the wind enables you to retrieve your fly with the current as if you are nymphing upstream.

to obtain consistency in the turnover of unusually long leaders. In this turnover, I am not trying to straighten the tippet, because slack there contributes to a fast sink rate through the first half-dozen feet of water.

The casting adjustments I make are generally in response to windy conditions. The most common adjustments are those needed to cast into the wind—tilting the casting plane for lower forward casts and using additional rod butt in the casting stroke.

Sometimes I find that the control of unusually long leaders is enhanced by maintaining a continuous motion from the back cast through the forward cast. This constant feeling of pressure from the line on the rod tip is obtained by making your back cast to the side and continuing the movement over the top on the forward cast. Lee and Joan Wulff have referred to this technique as "the Constant Pressure Oval," while Mel Krieger teaches it as the Belgian Cast in reference to its former use by tournament casters from Belgium. However named, it is also a useful cast when attempting to control heavy lines and large, weighted flies.

Figure 11.7 Fishing a floating line with a rod tip held just above the surface simplifies line control.

Line-Handling and Fishing Techniques

The best practitioners of this method are masters at retrieving the fly. Retrieves are sometimes based on careful study of the swimming movements of common lake insects (as observed in home aquariums), and developed by trial-and-error experimentation with various combinations of hand-twist or strip retrieves. Your movements of the artificial fly should be similar to those of the natural insect. The development of such retrieves may require the use of a swimming pool and a fishing buddy (i.e., someone else as wacky as you) to cast and retrieve while you watch the fly's movements.

When nymphing in lakes, the retrieve possibilities with floating lines and long leaders are different than those with most sinking lines. Though you can sink the fly well below the surface with either type of line, the floating line enables you to retrieve with small up and down movements of the fly throughout the drift.

Figure 11.8 A curve is formed in an unusually long leader that extends between floating line and weighted nymph. As you strip line, the fly moves upward and toward you. Between strips, the fly drops but continues toward you.

This resembles the preemergence movement of mayfly nymphs and midge pupae. On the other hand, most sinking lines tend to drag the fly along behind in a relatively horizontal plane until late in the drift when the movement is upward toward the tip of the rod.

When the fly has reached a depth of 10 feet with this rigging, a distinct downward curve has formed throughout the leader. Where it disappears below the surface, the leader is relatively horizontal; where it attaches to the fly, its tippet is nearly vertical. This vertical drop of the tippet positions the fly in a vertical, head-up posture regardless of where the weight is placed on the shank of the hook.

So, when you strip in a few inches of line, the fly moves upward and slightly toward you. Between strips, the fly descends toward the bottom and again somewhat toward you. The deeper the fly, the more vertical this movement is. Your best control of

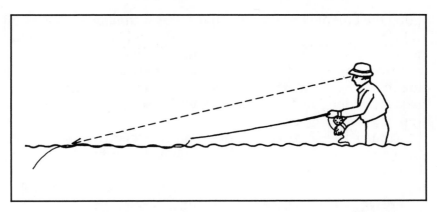

Figure 11.9   Watch the leader where it disappears into the depths for the first indication of a trout's take.

these movements occurs when your rod tip is held an inch or so above the water.

I mentioned that the depth you fish can be adjusted by varying the amount of weight on the nymph. It can be adjusted further by lengthening the tippet (for deeper drifts) or shortening it (for shallower drifts). Many anglers grease the leader butt instead of shortening the tippet, but Hal Janssen reports experiencing some spooking of fish by surface distortion created by the residue from the grease.

Hooking and Landing the Fish

In order to fish this method effectively, you must concentrate on the point at which your leader disappears into the water. If nothing happens, you begin to lose confidence and wonder if any fish are even in the area. For this reason, it is advisable to learn this method on a good, small lake, if one is available to you. At least then you know that trout are moving through the same piece of water you are casting into and fishing.

Quite often trout will take your fly while it is sinking, so any slowing or speeding in the sink rate of your leader is likely to indicate a taking fish. At this time you should set the hook by lifting the butt of your rod. If you fish this technique with a high rod tip, your tendency will be to pull the rod back toward you rather than upward on the strike, and you will break more tippets than you should. Again, remember to relax the grip on the line so it is free to slip through your line hand if the fish should make a sudden run. This adds further protection to your delicate tippet.

Trout in lakes sometimes grow to large sizes and can move with power and speed through still water. Such fish have potential to break the fine tippets by overrunning a low-quality reel. So for this method more than any other I have described, a relatively expensive, well-machined reel becomes important.

Wading and Safety

When carefully stalking trout by wading soft-bottomed lakes, you sometimes stand in one spot for several minutes without being aware that you have been sinking into the silt. You soon learn to withdraw your foot carefully to avoid losing balance and falling.

Variations of This Method

Far more has been written about stream fly fishing than about lake fly fishing. It seems our knowledge of lakes has lagged behind, partly because of the difficulty of drawing generalizations from bodies of water that are so different from one another.

Solving the problem of attracting trout in lakes may include a consideration of the interplay of variables such as time of day, time of year, weather, equipment, casting adjustments, available trout food, retrieve variations, and characteristics of the lake itself. The possibilities seem endless, which of course, contribute to the challenge and fascination of this form of angling.

Selected Readings

Clarke, B. (1975). *The pursuit of stillwater trout*. London: A. & C. Black.

Davy, A. (1985). *The gilly—A flyfisher's guide to British Columbia*. Altona, Manitoba, BC: D.W. Friesen & Sons, Ltd.

Janssen, H. (1980). The basic necessities. In J. Merwin (Ed.), *Stillwater trout*. Garden City, NY: Doubleday.

Janssen, H. (1980). The nymph in stillwater. In J. Merwin (Ed.), *Stillwater trout*. Garden City, NY: Doubleday.

Janssen, H. (1981, Pre-Season). Chironomidae: A moveable feast for stillwater trout. *Fly Fisherman*.

Janssen, H. (1981). Stillwater secrets—Insects, imitations, and fly lines. In Scientific Anglers (Ed.), *Fly Fishing Handbook*. Point Pleasant, NJ: Aqua–Field.

Shaw, J. (1980). *Fly fish the trout lakes*. Canada: Mitchell Press.

Chapter 12

Beyond Fly Fishing Methods: Adapting and Problem-Solving

Some years ago several friends joined me for an annual three-day fishing trip to the Sacramento and McCloud Rivers and Hat Creek. On that trip I didn't fish any differently than usual, but I did encounter more large fish that were willing to open their mouths at the wrong time. As a result I caught fish between 15 and 20 inches long on five of the methods described in this book. But I wasn't trying to catch fish on different methods. I was merely adapting my fishing to the variety of water I saw. And to me this *ability to adapt* is what differentiates the "hacker," and even the specialist, from a more complete fly fisherman. I believe it is what you should be working toward when you first practice fishing a method. Frank Collin paid me a great compliment not long ago in saying that what most characterizes my fly fishing is versatility—the ability to do very different things with a fly rigging to keep catching some trout under widely differing conditions. While I do love to experiment, changing riggings frequently sometimes keeps me from catching as many trout as I could.

Figure 12.1   When you begin to develop distinctive fishing operations for favorite pools or runs, you have gone well beyond fishing a method.

"Fishing a method" until you catch fish is an important process that enables you to gain confidence in a new set of fly fishing techniques. When you have confidence in your ability to use the techniques of that method, you are ready to incorporate the method into your fishing repertoire and use it situationally as you come upon the right kind of water for it. So when you practice fishing a given method, the method determines the water you fish. But when you are adapting to the water being fished, the water determines the method you select and helps you to develop specific adaptations in that method.

For example, let's imagine that you are about to fish a stream that has sections of pocket water. If you decide to fish a pocket-water method and you are in the early stages of learning it, you will repeat the same set of operations throughout the day, such as finding midstream rocks, positioning yourself, and casting into the slow water behind each one. You may even choose to pass up good water that doesn't suit a pocket-water method in order to concentrate on mastering one technique at a time and making it your own. However, with added confidence you will most likely fish through the various types of water you encounter and, when coming across pocket water, will quickly make the rigging and technique adjustments necessary to fish it well. Eventually, through trial and error learning, you pick up further refinements in your pocket-water technique from subtle differences among the short pools themselves. At this point you have begun to consider the extent to which each pool is unique. You have begun to develop distinctive fishing operations for each of your favorite pools and runs. Obviously you have gone well beyond fishing a method.

Even the same piece of water must be fished differently at times. For instance, I remember a day when my "program" didn't produce on one of my favorite runs at Hat Creek, where small dries or nymphs usually provide a fish or two for me. My good friend, Chet Murphy was across stream from me where he could see the two fish I was casting over. Occasionally he would inform me that the smaller fish had moved toward one of my size 16 nymphs or dry flies, but the larger fish continued to remain motionless two feet below the surface.

After half an hour, Chet suggested I try a large dry fly, because he had the impression that the small flies weren't drawing the trout's interest. Usually a large dry fly doesn't pay off during the midday hours at Hat Creek, but because I was short on ideas, I tied on a size 10 Elk Hair Caddis. The only large insects I had seen that morning were alder flies on some streamside foliage, so I blackened the caddis pattern with a felt pen. The larger fish, which hadn't moved a muscle for at least 30 minutes, rose quickly and surely to my first cast. Chet hung around long enough to make certain I returned his new "friend" to the stream.

Students often ask how I decide what methods or flies to use when first rigging up for a day's fishing. If the stretch of water is known to me, I usually start at an "indicator pool" that I know holds trout. Assuming there is no appreciable surface feeding, I generally begin fishing there with a deep nymph. If a fish takes the fly decisively, my first indication is that the fish are active and thus vulnerable to whatever fly fishing method or technique seems best suited to the conditions. I may even be able to enjoy the scenery around me and catch fish without expending much energy (anglers are like trout). However, if I get only a faint "bump" or no strike at all, my first indication is that the fish are not active and that I should continue to fish my fly deep and cover the water thoroughly, using techniques and fly patterns described in chapters 5, 7, or 10. This fishing will require my complete concentration. Of course, each pool I fish either modifies or further confirms this first impression.

But what techniques or flies do I start with on water I haven't fished before? Though I may be influenced by rumors and information I have gathered about that water, I typically make my fishing decisions only after parting the last alder branches and viewing the water. If fish are neither rising nor visible, I do what most experienced fly fishers do—begin "searching" operations.

For me, searching consists of finding where the trout are, or ought to be, and surmising which flies they are most likely to take. I try to zero in on the solution to these queries as quickly as possible, and use two types of techniques to do it—those that "double," in other words, cover two or more options, and those that permit quick rigging changes. Among the doubling techniques I have mentioned are selecting impressionistic flies that represent several types of insects and using two such flies at once to represent more insects as well as to sample two different depths simultaneously.

In some forms of doubling, the two (or more) options are covered on successive casts rather than on the same cast. Working up through a long run by alternating between short-line and long-line fishing is an example of this form of doubling. You may even select an initial stretch of stream that includes several types of water. This way you will sometimes find out quickly that trout are more active in certain types of water than in others. On lakes you may alternate between two different retrieves and use a "count" system to sample different depths.

I have also mentioned several techniques that permit you to change riggings quickly. I mentioned the loop system with interchangeable tippets to change leader length, removable split shot to change weight, and extra reel spools or extra shooting tapers to change fly lines. The sooner you find where the fish are active and what they will take, the more time remains to fish effectively.

Sometimes that first glimpse of water reveals rising trout. While you no longer have to find active fish, you still must determine what fly they will take. This last part of the puzzle can be

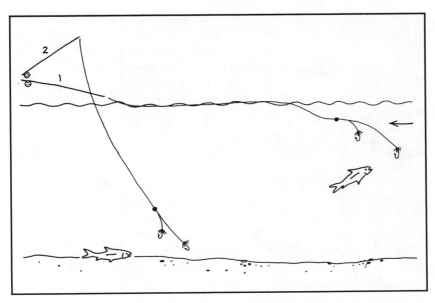

Figure 12.2   Nymphing up through a pool by alternating between long-line (1) and short-line (2) presentations is one form of "doubling." Fishing two different flies is another.

difficult to solve, particularly if the trout are taking only one stage (e.g., emerging nymphs) of one species of insect. What I do first in this situation is watch the trout rise. If I see an insect, such as a floating mayfly, drifting downstream, I watch to see if it gets inhaled by a trout. If it does, I grab the next drifting mayfly, hold it in hand to examine the color of the underside of its body (the side the trout sees) and tie on a dry fly to match its size, shape, and color. This is the most direct form of "matching the hatch."

Even when you don't see an insect eaten, the way a trout rises can provide clues to its feeding. As Bob Dering puts it, you may then be able to "match flies to the rise." If a small bubble is visible after the rise or if you see the trout's mouth break through, it has taken something off the surface and can be caught on a dry fly. However, if you see only the back or tail of the rising fish, or the water merely swirls or "bulges," the chances are the trout is taking its food, such as emerging mayfly nymphs, just below the surface. When you see splashy, explosive rises, the trout is generally chasing fast-moving food, such as a minnow or an emerg-

Figure 12.3   Seeing trout take an insect off the surface creates excitement and solves problems.

Figure 12.4   A trout changing position near the surface makes it tilt a little, which may appear as a sudden patch of light in dark water.

Figure 12.5 Sift the drift: Seining the surface drift frequently discloses the presence of barely submerged trout food.

ing caddis pupa. Quiet sipping by cruising fish, often in well established patterns, suggests food that is small, abundant, and vulnerable, such as tiny drifting mayfly "spinners" or midge pupae. A fish rising against a bank or under an overhanging tree or bush is often feeding on wind-blown land insects such as ants or grasshoppers.

It isn't always possible to tell from the "rise form" what a trout is eating, especially on broad stretches of water. So the next procedure I recommend is to wade downstream of the feeding trout without disturbing it and seine for drifting insects—"sift the drift." My seine is nothing more than a 12- by 18-inch piece of fine-mesh, fiberglass window screen with lengths of quarter-inch dowel rod taped to the shorter sides. This seine can be rolled up compactly until needed. I have found seining to be particularly enlightening when trout are taking food such as mayfly spinners and emerging pupae that are flush in the surface film and practically invisible to the naked eye.

Even your seine won't always solve the problem of what rising trout are eating. One day on the headwaters of the McCloud River, I was intrigued by a small trout that rose steadily in a quiet pool. I was still more intrigued after seining downstream of the fish without collecting so much as a single insect. I went back to fishing, without having solved the problem. Finally I caught that 9-inch trout, perhaps by irritating it. What I found was that it had been gorging on water boatmen, small water bugs that can rise vertically to get bubbles of air from the surface and swim back to their cover without being swept downcurrent to be inspected by cagey anglers.

A more typical stumbling block to using a seine is the presence of deep, unwadable water downstream of the rising trout. Somehow it seems that whenever deep water prevents me from using the seine, every visible insect is drifting well out of reach. With an esophagus pump, a suction device that samples the food a trout has just eaten, you may be able to "reveal the meal." These pumps can damage a trout fatally, though, unless used with very little suction. Of course, even a pump can't help if you haven't caught at least one of the rising fish.

So observing rise forms, manipulating seine, using binoculars to watch drifting insects, and other "intelligence gathering" may leave you where you started—with no direct knowledge of what the trout are eating.

Resist for a little longer the urge to break the fly rod over your knee. The clues may have told you enough to select fly patterns logically—by the process of elimination. If you don't see upwing mayflies (duns) on the water, or if those you see are not being eaten, eliminate from consideration all your standard dry flies with upright wings. If some part of the fish is breaking the surface, eliminate weighted nymphs unless you are fishing them downstream and swinging them up to the surface. So your selection of flies has been limited to those designed to float down in the film—emerging nymphs and pupae and downwing dries such as adult caddis, mayfly spinners, small adult stoneflies, and ants. The main thing I have found from checking the food eaten by evening-caught, meadow-stream trout is that these fish are selective, but not to the degree you might have expected. Their selectivity is frequently based on insect size and level of drift rather than on particular species of insect. So the patterns I would start with in this situation are rather small (size 14 or 16) and fished in or just below the surface film. If this doesn't solve the problem, and you still aren't able to "deduce the abstruse," the time may have come to break that fly rod. Just don't break mine.

This subtle form of torture, matching the hatch, can become highly addictive. Many of the better players of this game are so addicted that they have uprooted themselves from city lives and found ways to reside close to noteworthy streams. Even if you are not driven to follow their example, you may want to get closer to the life of streams by taking up the study of aquatic entomology and relating that knowledge to fly tying. You can even bring the stream home with you by setting up an entomology aquarium to hatch out insect specimens for convenient observation. If the scientific side is not appealing, you can bypass the study of insects and focus on specific fly hatches and use a limited number of well established patterns. Many fly fishers use this approach at places like Henry's Fork in Idaho. They return each year at the same time when the patterns they successfully used in previous years should still be effective. If something has changed, they are quick to pounce on tackle shop owners and knowledgeable friends for the most current information and the "hot" patterns. They enjoy a sense of self-worth without having to spend much time delving into the intricacies of the sport.

Whether you have been matching the hatch for years or are looking forward to your first fly fishing trip, it's exciting to learn new things about fly fishing. Each stream or lake you visit, each day you string up a rod, and each trout that follows your fly has the potential to add something to your storehouse of knowledge and to your pleasure. It is infinitely more exciting to me to catch a few fish by doing something new and different than to catch 50 or 100 trout doing something I already know.

I guess the most appealing thing to me about fly fishing is that there is so much to it. I have enjoyed learning to fly fish for 40 years and will be learning as long as the good Lord blesses me with the health to do it. Not long ago, my friend Scott Henderson jokingly asked me why I frequently put myself in the position of being outfished on "someone else's" stream. I answered that I like to learn new techniques and new waters, and don't mind even if my host takes the most productive spots. He knows the river and how to fish it most efficiently. Besides, the alternative is to bring him to my water, and use techniques I already know. I'd probably catch most of the fish that way, but I wouldn't learn much.

At this point, I'm looking forward to next season and that first day on the stream. I can't wait to find out what I don't know and what I'm going to learn next. Perhaps it will be a different wrinkle on a fishing technique or a better way to communicate that special feel of fly casting. Whatever it is, the chances are it won't have a dramatic effect on the number of fish I catch— particularly during those slow periods when trout keep their mouths closed. Every skilled fly fisherman I have watched has those periods when the time between fish is painfully long, and all he can do is present the fly well and occasionally change patterns or techniques. I mention this because too often the better fishermen among us leave the impression that they are always having those "hot moments" we sometimes witness. It simply isn't true. So just because you're not catching fish, don't conclude that you're fishing poorly. It may be the trout's fault.

What we learn on trout water sometimes has nothing to do with fishing technique. Though often preoccupied in improving our fish-catching skills, we may come away instead with a deepened appreciation for those complex, differentiated worlds in which trout live. Perhaps over a streamside sandwich, we attempt to reconstruct the events that shaped the beautiful landscape before us. As we realize that many centuries are invested in the creation of such beauty, we gain a sense of its true value and become protective of it. Probably that very spot which inspires us today has survived into the present because someone else became protective and then did something about it.

Some years back, anglers began to recognize the wisdom of returning most of our best fish to the water to insure future populations of wild trout. But this concept of "catch and release" may be thought of as going beyond the fish itself. Neither the trout nor its environment must be killed.

I've seen great fly fishermen, but if asked to pick "the best fisherman," I would have to cast my vote for any angler who has worked actively to protect and maintain the trout water that remains. After all, this person has made it possible for you and me to find places to fish where wild trout still live. What we have learned from this example has a reach that goes far beyond the teaching of fly fishing methods.

Index

sensory organs, 21-22
trout's window, 136-137
Trout water
availability of food, 22, 25-26, 45-46,
70, 122, 169-170, 186-191
bottom pockets, 67
cover, 21, 30, 46, 132-133
current deflection, 53-54, 133
current speed and depth, 67-68, 106, 132
current variation and pool size, 106
oxygen content, 20-21
reading the water, 22, 88, 104-105, 121,
132-133, 157, 184-186
water clarity, 44-45, 136
water temperature, 20-21
Truckee River, 62

U

Upper Sacramento River, 114, 125, 126, 183

W

Wading and safety equipment
felt or Ozite carpeting soles, 65, 78, 114
float tube, 51, 97, 174
flotation vest, 78
metal-bottomed footwear, 77-78
waders, 37, 51, 78-79, 113
wading shoes, 78, 114
wading staff, 78, 114, 128
Wading and safety situations
basic instruction, 37, 65
footwork, 114, 128, 136, 180
log jams, 65
meadow stream banks, 146

planning escape routes, 165-166
slippery or uneven rocks, 65, 114
wading carelessly, 113-114
wading wet and hypothermia, 37, 51
Water types
bait holes, 166-167
glides, 67, 117, 151
narrow pools, 117, 163
pocket water, 53-54, 99-100, 104-105
quiet meadow streams, 21, 131-133, 136,
150
riffles, 21, 25, 27, 30, 31, 38, 57, 67, 117,
126, 151
tailouts, 78
Weight on leader or fly, 27, 69-70, 71, 85,
100, 106, 108, 151, 155, 173, 179
Wet fly fishing techniques
below a floating line in lakes, 169-174
Brooks' method, 73-74, 80
down and across swing, 25
interaction of line-control, naturalness,
and depth, 99, 110-111, 150, 156, 161,
177
pocket water, 53
sinking line fishing in lakes, 83-87
upstream nymphing, 104, 149, 176
Whitlock, D., 22, 24, 168
Williamson River, 67
Wilson, D., 129
Wilson, H., 19
Wind, 48-49, 62, 88, 93, 140, 159, 170, 176
Wixom, H., 81
Wright, L., 146-147
Wulff, J., 19, 176
Wulff, L., 176

About the Author

Al Kyte, EdD, teaches physical activity and theory classes for the Department of Physical Education at the University of California, Berkeley, where he has been a faculty member for 25 years. He received his doctorate from Berkeley; as an undergraduate, he played basketball under the legendary Pete Newell and was an All-Conference first baseman in baseball.

Over the years, Al has become a popular speaker for many fly fishing clubs. For more than a decade of teaching and service, the Diablo Valley Fishermen (one of California's largest fly fishing clubs) named him ''Man of the Year.'' Al also teaches fly fishing classes through the University of California Extension, the prestigious Fenwick Fly Fishing Schools, and through his own fly fishing schools.

Al has authored articles for professional journals as well as popular fly fishing publications. In addition to his fly fishing interests, he enjoys coaching youth teams in basketball and baseball and is an avid naturalist. Al resides in Moraga, California, with his wife Barbara and their children, John and Tamara.